2 COMMAS

2
Commas

The founder's guide to exits,
building wealth and achieving freedom

Josh Comrie

First published in 2025 by Hambone Publishing
www.hambonepublishing.com.au

Editing by Mish Phillips and Felicity Harrison
Cover design by Larch Gallagher
Interior design by David W. Edelstein

For information about this title, contact:
Josh Comrie
josh@joshcomrie.com

ISBN 978-1-922357-98-4 (paperback)
ISBN 978-1-922357-99-1 (ebook)
ISBN 978-1-922357-10-6 (audiobook)

Contents

Prologue

"*The cave you fear to enter holds the treasure you seek.*"

– Joseph Campbell

WHY THIS BOOK EXISTS

What if the exit isn't the end, but the beginning?

Most founders don't start companies because they want to sell them.

They start because they're excited, curious, stuck, broke, naïve, stubborn – or all of the above.

But every business, whether you realise it or not, is heading toward an end.

That end might be a sale, a merger, a handover, a burnout, a fizzle... or potentially, a funeral.

This book is about getting ahead of that moment – so you don't stumble into it the way so many do.

What it's not is a how-to-sell-your-business checklist. You can Google that.

This is a book about **how to exit well**, and **feel good about it afterwards.**

It's about how to think, not just what to do. It's about shifting from reactive to intentional. From default to design.

It's about the ten invisible decisions you're making right now that are already shaping your eventual outcome; consciously or otherwise.

And yes, it's about money.

But it's also about freedom, identity, timing, power... and regret.

WHY IT'S CALLED "2 COMMAS"

The quick among you will have established that "2 Commas" references seven figures. It also captures eight and nine, i.e. everything up to $999,999,999 – basically $1 billion. At the time of writing, this is still considered a huge achievement – the kind of exits people whisper about behind your back and podcast hosts crawl over each other for an exclusive on.

Having been around hundreds of exits now, one thing I know for sure is that **the money isn't the endgame.** It's just a chapter. And a comma signals that there's something about to come after it.

In 2024, I kicked off a podcast with the same name, focused on exits. The podcast took off faster than I ever expected, because we aren't just talking about deals. We're talking about the journey, the trials and tribulations and, of course, what comes next – the untold stories behind the exits. The moments of reckoning, reinvention, and, sometimes, a dose of resentment and remorse.

What I've learned from those conversations – and from living this journey myself – is simple:

A great exit isn't just about wealth. It's about freedom. It's about building something that lasts, and stepping away in a way that leaves you whole.

This book is here to help you get that right – the commas and the life on the other side of them.

It's about helping you design a sale that feels like completion, not collapse.

One that delivers not just wealth – but agency.

Because with agency comes optionality. Clarity. And perhaps most importantly, **peace.**

WHO THIS IS FOR

If you're a founder with a decent business and a vague sense that you might want to sell one day, **this is for you.**

If you've already had people sniffing around your company and you're wondering what you should do about it, **this is for you.**

If you've sold already and are trying to figure out why it didn't feel like fireworks and freedom, **this is for you.**

And, if you're someone with the desire and hunger to start a business and want to know how to do this right from day one – **this is definitely for you.**

HOW TO USE THIS BOOK

You don't need to read it all at once.

But you *do* need to be honest with yourself as you go.

Each chapter starts with a big question – one you may not have asked yet, but you should.

You'll hear from other founders (real ones, not tech-bro Instagram "founders"), from M&A insiders, from a few philosophers, and from me – someone who's been through the full cycle more than once and has helped others do the same.

You'll get models, frameworks, metaphors, and the occasional uncomfortable truth.

You'll also get a roadmap that's flexible enough to fit your style, yet strong enough to keep you from falling into the same traps so many others do.

The book's architecture

This book is structured as a progressive journey through the four dimensions of an ideal strategic exit:

Part I: The Identity Dimension | Ownership & Letting Go

We begin where most exit books never venture: the psychology of ownership. You'll discover why many financially successful exits lead to founder regret, how your relationship with your business shapes your exit options, and why preparing for the identity shift is as crucial as preparing for the financial transaction. Through the stories of founders who've navigated this terrain, you'll gain insight into the invisible forces that can either sabotage or supercharge your exit.

Part II: The Value Dimension | Beyond Conventional Metrics

Next, we'll dismantle the myths of business valuation that cause founders to undervalue their companies. You'll learn why standard valuation methods are designed to benefit buyers, how strategic positioning can multiply your exit value regardless of financial performance, and why the concept of fair market value may be the most expensive illusion in business.

Part III: The Power Dimension | Controlling the Exit Dynamic

The third section exposes the hidden power dynamics that determine exit outcomes. You'll discover why founders unknowingly negotiate from a position of weakness, how sophisticated buyers exploit information asymmetries, and the counter-intuitive strategies that flip these dynamics in your favour.

Part IV: The Legacy Dimension | Engineering Your Next Chapter

Finally, we'll look beyond the transaction to ensure your exit
serves your broader life narrative. You'll explore why the true
measure of exit success isn't the purchase price but what the exit
enables, how to structure deals that secure both wealth and wellbeing, and the frameworks successful founders use to transition
from building companies to building legacies.

The format

Every chapter delivers a fresh lens and breakthrough clarity,
blending hard-won wisdom with actionable, strategic insights
that scale. Here's what makes the journey unique:

- **No Easy Questions:** Each chapter opens with pro-
  vocative questions that will challenge your status quo
  – questions that make you pause, reflect, and potentially
  reshape your entire exit strategy.

- **No Highlight Reels:** Forget sanitised success stories and
  PR spin. You'll hear the raw details of spectacular wins
  and crushing failures from founders who've been in the
  trenches – no filters here.

- **No Armchair Theory:** You'll gain access to the exact
  frameworks and decision models founders use to craft
  a successful exit. Not PowerPoint fluff – what actually works.

Each section concludes with a strategic **Checkpoint** – a
chance to step back, take stock of what you've learned, and
surface the uncomfortable truths about your business and exit
readiness – the blind spots that could cost you millions... and
your marbles.

You'll also find eye-opening **Founder Case Studies** through-out the book. Some smooth, some messy. A few might surprise you. All of them show the full gamut of what an exit can look like so you can spot the patterns – and dodge the pitfalls – in your own journey.

BEYOND INFORMATION: TRANSFORMATION

This book will transform how you perceive, prepare for, and execute your exit. The insights here stem from three decades in the entrepreneurial trenches: founding and selling five $multi-million dollar businesses, investing in over fifty start-ups, launching the 2 Commas podcast, and advising founders who've built billions in enterprise value. What separates those who capture extraordinary value from those who settle isn't just better tactics – **it's a fundamentally different understanding of what an exit is and how it unfolds.**

We'll begin by exploring the hidden psychological forces that shape your relationship with your business – forces that can either poison your exit or multiply its value.

The choice is yours. Let's begin.

Introduction

"*S*o... *I'm thinking about selling.*"
Stated in the first person, that sentence will either fill you with quiet excitement or a weird sensation in your chest you can't quite name. Maybe both.

For some founders, an exit is the goal from day one. Others just wake up one day, look at their calendar, and think, "I can't keep doing this." And the lucky, strategic, or well-advised manage to pull off something that changes their life in all the ways they hoped it would.

THE EXIT PARADOX

You're running a successful business.

You've crossed the seven-figure (or eight, even nine) revenue threshold. You've built a team that executes your vision. Your market position is solid, perhaps even dominant in your niche. By conventional standards, you've "made it" – you've overcome the 65 per cent failure rate that claims most businesses within seven years of starting.

Yet something remains *unresolved.*

In quiet moments – perhaps late at night when the emails stop, or on rare holidays when you briefly step away – a question surfaces that you quickly suppress:

"How does this story end?"

> *This is the exit paradox:*
> *the best time to design your exit*
> *is when you have no immediate*
> *intention to sell.*

Founders typically never ask this question until circumstances force them to confront it: a health scare, a competitive threat, an unsolicited offer – or worse, burnout. By then, options have narrowed, leverage has evaporated, and what could have been the crowning achievement of your entrepreneurial journey becomes a compromised conclusion to years of sacrifice.

This is the exit paradox: the best time to design your exit is when you have no immediate intention to sell.

Let me tell you about two people who faced this on very different terms.

Tim built his company from scratch. Big revenue, decent team, looked good from the outside. But behind the scenes, cracks were forming. He'd scaled fast, outgrown parts of his leadership, and had started drifting away from the business without realising it. Eventually, a banker came knocking at the right (or wrong) time, and Tim said yes. Not because he was ready – because he was tired.

It wasn't a terrible exit. But it wasn't on his terms.

It was a reaction, not a decision.

Then there's Sharon. She'd also built her company from

scratch and enjoyed an exciting ride: multiple markets, amazing products, an award-winning business. She woke up one day and said, "I'm done, I need to replace myself." So she hired a professional CEO whose mandate was to continue growth then sell the company. From day one, the founders, board, and new CEO were aligned. Every move Sharon made was filtered through that lens: how do we grow this in a way that makes it both valuable and saleable?

When Sharon sold, it was deliberate. Strategic. On her timeline.

Tim's exit was at a four-times EBITDA multiple, and left him exhausted.

Sharon's was ten times – and she'd left the building two years earlier. No scrambling, no guessing, no regrets.

Both Tim and Sharon had high-growth, profitable, competitively leading businesses. Similar age, scale, and stage. From the outside, not dissimilar assets.

These are two very different endings.

And two very different beginnings.

THE SILENT WEALTH TRANSFER

When you build a business without designing its ending, you unwittingly participate in one of the largest wealth transfers in business: from founder to acquirer.

The mechanics of this transfer are subtle but systematic.

The average founder spends over 40,000 hours building their business before exit, yet they'll dedicate less than 100 hours to planning how that exit unfolds. This asymmetry of attention creates a dangerous vulnerability that sophisticated buyers are well-positioned to exploit.

Buyers aren't evil or malicious; they're rational. They're professionally incentivised to acquire your business for the lowest possible price, on terms most favourable to them. Often, they conduct dozens of acquisitions. They employ teams of professionals whose sole purpose is to optimise deal structures. They possess market data you simply don't have.

You, meanwhile, will sell your business **exactly once.**

This imbalance leads to a predictable outcome: the systematic transfer of wealth from founders who built companies to acquirers who buy them – a transfer that often reaches 30–50 per cent of a business's true value.

FREEDOM: THE ULTIMATE CURRENCY

Why did you start your business?

If you're like the majority of founders I've worked with, your answer wasn't "to maximise EBITDA" or "to optimise my exit valuation". You started your business to create freedom – the freedom to control your time, make your own decisions, build something meaningful, and eventually achieve financial independence.

Yet, ironically, as your business grows, freedom often diminishes. The larger your company becomes, the more stakeholders depend on you, the greater your responsibilities, and, paradoxically, the less freedom you experience. What began as a vehicle for independence becomes a constraint.

This is the entrepreneur's dilemma: **the very success you've worked for can become the cage that traps you.**

An exit – when executed strategically – isn't merely a financial transaction. It's your path back to freedom: not just financial freedom, but freedom of time, purpose, and identity.

*An exit that maximises valuation
but compromises your freedom
isn't a successful exit at all.*

Freedom to choose your next chapter without the constraints of your current one.

An exit that maximises valuation but compromises your freedom isn't a successful exit at all.

THE FOUNDER BLIND SPOT

Let me be blunt about something most business books won't tell you: the biggest obstacle to your successful exit isn't market conditions, industry multiples, or buyer behaviour.

It's **you** – your attachment, your identity, your ego, your fear, your capability, your optimism.

Johari's Window is a powerful psychological framework revealing four quadrants of self-awareness. There's **what you know about yourself, what others know about you, what everyone knows,** and – most dangerously during exits – **what no one knows,** including you. These unknown aspects drive decisions in ways you can't recognise without deliberate reflection.

My experience shows that your psychology drives your exit outcomes more than any other factor. The vast majority of founders operate with significant blind spots – unable to see patterns in their own decision-making, emotional triggers, and unconscious biases about value, timing, and leverage.

The most dangerous negotiator isn't across the table – it's the one you can't see in the mirror.

I've seen it repeatedly: founders with the business acumen to build eight-figure companies suddenly make irrational decisions when their identity is threatened, their control is challenged, or their deep attachments to their creation are tested. The exit process doesn't just evaluate your business; it reveals your relationship with yourself.

These patterns remain unseen by you but painfully obvious to experienced buyers. This is why the most successful exits are financially engineered *after* they're psychologically engineered.

The most dangerous negotiator isn't across the table – it's the one you can't see in the mirror.

THE STRATEGIC EXIT BLUEPRINT

This book deliberately breaks from conventional business literature. I've personally built and exited multiple ventures, and guided hundreds of founders through scaling and many to successful exits. I've observed that those who capture the most value don't just follow better procedures; they operate from an entirely different mental model.

What you'll find here isn't a simplistic roadmap. The exit landscape is too complex, the stakes too high, and your business too unique for cookie-cutter solutions. Plus, DIY exits invariably leave substantial value (often millions) on the table. Don't do this.

Instead, this book provides something far more valuable: **a complete reconceptualisation of what an exit actually is** and how the most successful founders approach it.

WHAT'S REALLY AT STAKE

Let's talk numbers for a moment. A typical founder exit in the seven- or eight-figure range can vary by 30–50 per cent based on how it's approached, negotiated, and structured. These aren't rounding errors – they're life-changing sums.

And the financial gap is just the beginning. I've seen too many founders achieve their "number" only to discover that the deal structure leaves them trapped in a role they've outgrown, reporting to people they don't respect, or tied to earn-out metrics they can no longer influence.

I've also seen founders walk away with significant wealth and a deep sense of fulfilment, purpose, and freedom – not just because they got a good price, but because they approached the entire process with clarity about what success truly meant for them.

The gap between these outcomes isn't luck. It's strategy. It's preparation. It's perspective. **And that's what this book delivers.**

BEYOND THE TRANSACTION

If you're the type of person who reads prologues, you'll already be familiar with the four dimensions of an ideal strategic exit that guide this book. If you're not, no worries, but I do encourage you to have a flip back to the Prologue before considering the following thematic questions. It's my hope that these reflections will help you get nicely warmed up to the meat and potatoes to follow.

1. The Identity Dimension

Who are you beyond your founder role? How will you maintain purpose and meaning after the exit? What's your relationship with success, wealth, and status?

2. The Value Dimension

What is your business truly worth – not just by conventional metrics but to specific strategic buyers? How do you position your company to capture its maximum value?

3. The Power Dimension

How do you maintain negotiating leverage? How do you create competitive tension among multiple acquirers so the outcome isn't determined by who needs the deal more?

4. The Legacy Dimension

How do you structure a deal that protects what matters most post-acquisition? How do you prepare your team, culture, and customers for transition and maintain influence where it counts? How do you secure your wellbeing, not just your wealth?

Founders tend to focus exclusively on #2 while completely neglecting the other three dimensions. The result? Deals that look good on paper but **feel hollow in reality.** Transactions that optimise for price while **compromising everything else that matters**.

The founders who execute truly successful exits address all four dimensions with *equal strategic discipline*. They recognise that the exit is not just a financial event, but a complex transition that affects every aspect of their lives and legacy.

This book is your guide to exiting by design – ensuring your exit becomes not just a lucrative transaction, but a transformative transition into your most meaningful work.

THE EXIT CHOICE: DEFAULT OR DESIGN

Every founder will eventually exit. The only question is whether that exit happens by default or by design.

Exits by default are reactive – driven by burnout, market pressure, competitive threats, or unsolicited offers. They're characterised by compressed timelines, limited options, and outcomes that fall far short of potential.

Exits by design are proactive – built on strategic preparation, psychological readiness, and deliberate timing. They're characterised by multiple options, strong negotiating leverage, and outcomes that maximise both financial returns and personal freedom.

The difference isn't forged in the final negotiation; it's forged years earlier – in how you build and position your business, and how you prepare yourself for the inevitable transition.

This book is your guide to exiting by design – ensuring your exit becomes not just a lucrative transaction, but a transformative transition into your most meaningful work.

The exit isn't the end of your story. It's the moment you receive new resources to write a more meaningful chapter. Make sure it's a chapter worth reading.

PART I

The Identity Dimension

OWNERSHIP AND LETTING GO

The exit is about you, not your business

CHAPTER 1

When Ego Kills Deals

*"The most important decision for an
entrepreneur is knowing when to quit."*

– Naval Ravikant

*"We sort of had no desire to sell – until we did quite
quickly… We were just young and weren't able to
step back and be strategic. It's a regret of mine."*

– Tim, Founder

Could you walk away from your company without feeling like you're giving up part of yourself?

. . . .

*In 2019, life couldn't have been better for Adam Neumann.
His 9-year-old startup, WeWork, had peaked at a staggering
$47 billion valuation, with his personal stake valuing him in the
billions. He'd been named one of TIME's genius entrepreneurs
of the year in 2018, appeared on the cover of Forbes, and was
hailed as a visionary reshaping the future of work. Celebrities,
tech giants, and venture capitalists all wanted a piece of his*

> *What looked like a business*
> *failure was, at its core,*
> *an identity failure.*

world – and SoftBank's Masayoshi Son had handed him a blank cheque, calling him a once-in-a-generation founder.

WeWork's rapid rise seemed unstoppable, and Neumann was at the centre of it all, boldly declaring: "We are here in order to change the world. Nothing less than that interests me."

Then within short months, it all began to unravel...

Somewhere along the way, the line between Adam Neumann and WeWork disappeared completely. His personal brand, lifestyle, and ego became indistinguishable from the company's identity. Private jets. Tequila-fuelled meetings. Grandiose proclamations about "elevating the world's consciousness". Unconstrained hallucinations masquerading as strategy.

When it came time for the public markets to evaluate WeWork, they weren't just examining a business model – they were judging a founder who couldn't distinguish himself from his creation. The consequence was a plummeting valuation; from $47 billion to nearly zero, forcing Neumann out and leaving the startup in chaos.

What looked like a business failure was, at its core, an identity failure.

Contrast this with Mihail and Georgi, founders of SMS Bump and NitroPack. These founders never actually planned their exits. Instead, they focused relentlessly on building efficient, profitable businesses that solved specific problems exceptionally well.

When opportunity knocked, they were ready – not because they were desperate to sell, but because they were clear-eyed about the value they'd created and what it was worth to strategic acquirers.

Their approach began years before any acquisition talks. SMS Bump started with a simple integration request that laid the groundwork for a relationship with eventual acquirer Yotpo. NitroPack leveraged strategic partnerships as "Trojan horses", allowing potential acquirers to experience their value first-hand.

The combined value of their exits was over $3 billion.

The difference wasn't just in their businesses. It was in how they related to those businesses. They maintained the psychological separation between themselves and their companies – seeing them as valuable creations rather than extensions of their identities.

Which brings me to the uncomfortable truth that founders never want to hear, but that Mihail and Georgi understood instinctively.

THE INVISIBLE FORCE IN EVERY EXIT

You are the biggest risk to your exit.
Not the market.
Not the buyer.
Not your EBITDA.

You.

Not because you're not smart.

Not because you don't care.

But because somewhere along the way, **you became your business.** Like Adam Neumann – but hopefully with fewer messiah-like hallucinations.

*The buyer feels it
before they see it.*

It happens to all of us.

You put in the years. The weekends. The grey hairs. You fought for the first sale, the first hire, the first real month of profit. And somewhere in that long grind, the business stopped being **a thing you built** – and became **who you are.**

Which is fine – until it's time to sell. Or hire your replacement...

Rookie founders don't realise what happens when you walk into that first serious buyer meeting: they're not leading with spreadsheet analysis. Buy-side teams are shrewd professionals who double as polished amateur psychologists. They're reading **you** before they're reading your numbers.

The buyer feels it before they see it.

One of the biggest things buyers evaluate – quietly, subconsciously – is **founder energy.**

Are you clear? Calm? Ready to transition?

Or are you clinging to the business like a life raft?

> *You lose leverage the moment*
> *you lose clarity.*

They can tell.

They *always can.*

Here's the reality: most strategic buyers aren't just buying a business. They're buying **optionality**. If they sense you're not ready to step away – or worse, that you'll (even unintentionally) sabotage the handover – they'll walk. Or they'll discount the offer to compensate.

You lose leverage the moment you lose clarity.

> **Perceived business risk =**
> **actual business risk x founder attachment**

You can have perfect financials, growing market share, and a bulletproof business model. But if the buyer senses you're emotionally erratic, defensive, or lost without the business? They assume there's something you're not telling them.

They price that uncertainty straight into the deal.

HOW IT PLAYS OUT: THREE REAL STORIES

Meredith – The Validation Seeker

. . . .

Meredith spent eight years building a virtual fitness coaching platform service into something wonderful. Customer loyalty was strong, operations were smooth, growth was steady. When a strategic buyer approached, she'd already fixated on one very specific, very round number – her "life-changing" exit figure.

Just post the Covid lockdowns an offer came in - at 80% of that number. And, it was a revenue multiple! Not EBITDA – unusual for the businesses model and generous given the market timing. Her advisors were excited. Market forces were shifting against virtual coaching models, and deals like this were becoming rare.

"It's not enough," Meredith said. "They don't understand what we've built here."

The buyer tried explaining the premium they were paying, the strategic value they saw, the market conditions making similar deals unlikely. Meredith heard none of it. The number felt like a personal judgment on her worth.

She walked away.

Three years later, she's still trying to find another buyer willing to pay even close to that original offer. Post Covid, online fitness coaching has tanked, multiples have compressed, and what seemed like a lowball offer now looks like the deal of a lifetime.

The buyer wasn't rejecting Meredith's worth as a person. They were offering fair market value at a moment when the market was about to turn. She couldn't separate her ego from economic reality.

Steve – The Irreplaceable Hero

. . . .

Steve ran every client relationship personally. "They buy from me, not the company," he'd say proudly. When buyers saw this total founder dependency, they offered aggressive earn-outs and demanded two-year employment contracts.

Steve was insulted. "Don't they see I'm the whole reason this works?"

They did. That was exactly the problem.

He delegated little and when he did, he second guessed the decision. He inserted himself into every hiring process, but not performance management when things went wrong. He'd proclaim to new hires that "his DNA was stamped all over the company".

Troy – The Identity Defender

. . . .

Troy had been co-founder of a high-growth tech company. After four years, the founding CEO – who believed in the "zero-to-one" principle and knew his own limitations – handed leadership over to Troy for the scaling phase.

Then Troy flatlined the company's growth. Against a backdrop of incredible market opportunities, he floundered across multiple strategies, never committing fully to any single direction. The focused execution that had built early momentum dissolved into strategic confusion.

When a market timing opportunity finally opened up and buyers emerged, Troy started sabotaging his own process.

He'd miss due diligence deadlines, show up late to meetings, provide incomplete information for standard requests, and get defensive about basic questions every buyer asks.

His advisor finally confronted him: "Troy, do you actually want to sell?"

"Of course I do."

"Then why are you acting like you don't?"

The truth was more complicated. Troy had spent years being "CEO of TechCorp" after taking over from the founder. But deep down, he knew he'd failed to fulfil the potential that had been handed to him. The acquisition process felt like a public examination of his shortcomings as a leader.

So he subconsciously ensured the deal would collapse, protecting his bruised identity by destroying any chance of financial recovery.

Internal clarity creates external leverage.

THE DETACHMENT SOLUTION

A counterintuitive truth: the less emotionally dependent you are on a specific exit outcome, the better your outcome will likely be.

There's a critical distinction between **working toward** a specific number and **needing** that number to feel worthy, seen and validated. One gives you direction. The other gives you desperation.

Internal clarity creates external leverage.

WHAT HUMILITY ACTUALLY LOOKS LIKE

The founders who stop death-gripping the particulars of their exit tend to negotiate the strongest ones. I'm not suggesting you abandon targets. Business owners are goal-setters by nature – it's what built your company. But aiming for a number and being emotionally dependent on it are two ends of the yardstick. One gives you direction, the other gives you desperation. This isn't philosophy; it's practical psychology with tangible financial consequences.

When you're clear-eyed about who you are – separate from your business – you gain:

1. **Negotiation leverage:** You can credibly walk away, which is the strongest position in any deal

2. **Decision clarity:** You evaluate options based on merit, not emotional need

3. **Timing power:** You can wait for the right moment, not be forced by burnout or desperation

4. **Presence magnetism:** You project the calm confidence that makes buyers want to close

Clarity compounds.

Humility isn't what you think it is

Humility gets confused with weakness in deal-making. It's actually a superpower.

Real humility in an exit looks like swallowing your pride when you don't know something instead of winging it. It's hearing criticism of your baby without losing your mind. It's axing projects you love that buyers see as distractions. It's paying for advisors to tell you hard truths, not comfortable lies.

You're not surrendering. You're being strategically smart when your financial future is on the line.

Buyers pay more for founders who've already made peace with leaving. They lean in when they meet someone who's proud of what they've built but doesn't need the business to feel whole.

That's when they trust the numbers. That's when they move faster. That's when you keep control – precisely because you're not grasping for it.

The process begins with a simple but confronting question: who would you be if this business disappeared tomorrow?

Not your assets or reputation. YOU. What parts of your self-concept would survive? What parts would collapse?

For most of us, this question reveals uncomfortable gaps – places where you've outsourced your sense of self to something external and impermanent.

These gaps aren't weaknesses. They're opportunities for what psychologists call "differentiation" – the healthy separation between who you are and what you do.

This differentiation isn't merely philosophical – it's practical. I've seen it add seven figures to exit valuations by giving founders the psychological freedom to walk away from bad deals, patiently build competitive tension, and present themselves as assets rather than dependencies.

✔ CHECKPOINT: ARE YOU SELLING... OR ESCAPING?

Before you move on, sit with these five questions:

- If you weren't allowed to mention your company, how would you describe yourself?
- Are you hoping a buyer will fix your burnout – or reward your clarity?
- What part of the business would you find emotionally hard to hand over – and why?
- Are you overpricing the company to delay making the decision to sell?
- If the deal closed tomorrow, what would you do on Monday?
- You don't need perfect answers. But you do need honest ones.

Because if you want to sell your business without sabotaging it in the final mile, you have to know where you end, and the business begins.

CHAPTER 2

What Happens After You Get the Cash?

The identity crash no one prepares for

"Everything you've ever wanted is on the other side of fear."

– George Addair

What do you do when the main thing that defined you is suddenly gone?

The morning after the wire hits your account, you'll wake up a multimillionaire.

And you'll feel like shit.

Not immediately, perhaps. There might be a champagne-soaked celebration. A vacation. **The first genuine exhale in years.**

But then something unexpected happens: a disorienting stillness descends where there was once constant motion.

The emails stop. The Slack notifications go quiet. The urgent problems that structured your days disappear. The identity you've worn for years – sometimes decades – is suddenly an artefact. And the question that's been too busy to surface finally emerges:

"Who am I when I'm not the founder of my company?"

You're "done".

Now what?

If you're like most founders, no one prepared you for what happens next.

And I can share from my own experience – it's not just golf, vacations, LinkedIn glory, and passive income.

It's weird. It's quiet. It's existential.

THE CAPTAIN WITHOUT A SHIP

For years, you've been the captain of your vessel.

Every morning, you rise before dawn, step onto the bridge, and feel the familiar vibration of the engines beneath your feet. The crew looks to you for direction. The maps and instruments await your command. The horizon offers both challenge and possibility.

You knew where you were going (most days!). You had the shiny veneer of control.

Being the captain isn't just your job – it's your identity. The weight of the captain's hat has shaped you. The responsibility has defined you. The daily decisions have become the rhythm of your existence.

Then one day, you sign the papers. The transaction closes. The wire hits your account.

You step off the ship.

You stand on the shore, pockets full of gold, watching as your vessel – the one you designed, built, and commanded – disappears over the horizon without you. The crew still aboard. The engines still humming. The journey continuing.

But you remain on the shore.

The next morning comes, and there's no bridge to walk to.

No crew awaiting instruction. No course to chart. No purpose baked into the dawn.

Who are you now, Captain, without your ship?

. . . .

You go from being the centre of a universe to someone with a windfall and a blank calendar.

. . . .

This is the identity void that catches founders by surprise. All the money in your account can't buy you a new identity. So what actually happens to captains without ships?

The identity inversion:

You go from being the centre of a universe to someone with a windfall and a blank calendar.

But it's not just about losing your title. It's about losing the entire ecosystem that defined your days, piece by piece, until nothing familiar remains.

Your morning routine? Gone. Remember how you grabbed coffee from the energetic young team next door to the office, shared a joke and thought that you gave them hope into the future of self-employment? That daily connection, that small moment of mentorship and human warmth – vanished. Now you wake up and there's nothing urgent waiting, no familiar faces expecting you.

Your social circle has been transformed overnight in ways that feel surprisingly like death. For those colleagues and clients, in some ways you have died – the version of you they knew, the person who was always available for the next deal or crisis or strategic discussion. A part of you feels the same. You're mourning someone you used to be while trying to figure out who you are now.

The corner office or central cubicle you occupied, with its desk covered in personal trinkets and family photos? It's not yours anymore. Even your calendar – that tyrannical master that ruled your every hour for years, demanding you rush from meeting to meeting, deadline to deadline – sits empty. The same calendar you used to complain about, but secretly wore like a badge of honour. "I'm slammed this week," you'd say with that particular mixture of exhaustion and pride that only founders understand. Being busy meant you mattered. A packed schedule was proof of your importance, your indispensability, your success.

Now that calendar stares back at you, blank and accusatory. Your nervous system, wired for constant urgency and problem-solving, doesn't know what to do with the sudden stillness. There's no dopamine hit from juggling three calls while responding to urgent emails. No rush from being the person everyone needs right now. Your ego searches for the business card that used to define you, the one that opened doors and commanded respect at networking events.

Your body moves through days without structure, without the familiar rhythms that once anchored every hour – the morning sprint to make the first meeting, the working lunch that wasn't really a break, the evening calls with international clients that made you feel globally important. Being busy wasn't just what you did; it was *who you were*. And now, in the silence,

This is what I consider the complete structural collapse. It's not just losing your identity – it's losing the entire framework that held your life together.

you're forced to confront a terrifying question: if you're not busy, do you still matter?

This is what I consider the complete structural collapse. It's not just losing your identity – it's losing the entire framework that held your life together.

And when faced with this terrifying emptiness, unprepared founders almost always make the same mistakes. I've seen it hundreds of times – on the podcast, with founders I've worked with, and in my own journey.

THE FREEDOM PARADOX

It's a cruel irony: you built your company seeking freedom. You sold it to finally claim that freedom. But when the freedom arrives, it feels nothing like you imagined.

Instead of liberation, you feel adrift. Instead of satisfaction, you feel empty. Instead of clarity, you face the most profound question of your adult life: **now what?**

The freedom you fought so hard to achieve can feel like a void if you haven't prepared for it. From my own stumbles and

countless founder stories, I've seen how this void triggers surprisingly predictable reactions. Not because we're broken, but
because we're human. Let me share what I've learned...

WHY ENTREPRENEURIAL SUCCESS DOESN'T MAKE YOU BUFFETT

The first reaction I see all the time is cashed-up founders suddenly styling themselves as investors.

The logic seems sound.

> *"I built a successful company, so I must know how to spot
> other successful companies, right?"*

Wrong.

There's a halo effect at play here that trips up even the smartest founders. You assume the skills that made you successful as
an entrepreneur automatically translate to being a successful
investor. But building a company and evaluating companies
require completely different skill sets.

As an entrepreneur, you're intimately connected to the problem you're solving. You know your customers' pain points, your
market dynamics, your competitive landscape. You can pivot
when things aren't working because you understand every lever
in your business.

As an investor? You're placing bets on other people's understanding of problems you may know nothing about. You're
evaluating management teams from the outside, trying to
predict market trends in industries you've never operated in,
and hoping someone else can execute a vision you may not
fully grasp.

I watched this happen to a founder I'll call Matt. He'd sold his Engineering Consulting Company for well into eight figures – a genuine success story built over years of understanding his clients, refining his processes, and building deep relationships in his industry.

Within a year of his exit, Matt had written seven-figure cheques into three completely different industries. Tech, health-care, and retail – sectors he'd never worked in, with business models he'd never tested, solving problems he'd never faced personally. The initial confidence was intoxicating – finally, he could back other visionaries the way he'd once needed backing.

Then the quarterly reports started arriving… confidence turned to concern, then to growing panic as the numbers told a story he didn't want to believe. Two of those investments failed within three years. The third? It was haemorrhaging cash so badly that Matt had to write more cheques, step in and take over operations, essentially becoming an entrepreneur again but in an industry he didn't understand, with a much smaller equity stake, solving a problem he had no real connection to.

Matt learned the hard way that success in one arena doesn't automatically transfer to another – especially when ego clouds judgement. He went from being the expert in his field to being a novice in three new ones, trading his hard-earned expertise for the illusion of diversification.

I've been angel investing for over 25 years and done well over 50 deals, so I've seen this pattern play out countless times. Founders with fresh exit money suddenly styling themselves as "angel investors" without any real strategy or genuine passion for it – they're conflating investing for therapy.

They fill their calendars with pitch meetings and coffee chats, doing all that they can to recreate the feeling of relevance and value. Here's what they miss: when your advice is free and there's no real commitment from either party, founders don't value what you're offering. You end up becoming a slave to your calendar again – different meetings, same emptiness.

Right after selling my first company, despite an investment portfolio of 18 startups in my personal family office, I found myself in this exact trap.

Real angel investing isn't about filling time or feeling important. It's about deploying capital and expertise strategically toward founders and problems you genuinely care about. The difference between authentic investing and identity-driven busy work is obvious once you know what to look for.

Matt wasn't just making bad investments – he was trying to buy his way into a new identity without understanding what that identity actually required. But Matt wasn't alone in mistaking his exit for a license to transform his entire lifestyle.

WHEN MORE BECOMES THE NEW HIGH

The second pattern I see is founders developing what I call "substitute addictions". When the natural high of building a company disappears – the rush of closing deals, solving problems, being needed – they search desperately for new highs to fill that void.

What psychologists call hedonic adaptation kicks in. You've got money now, real money, so why not upgrade? Better house, better car, better vacations.

It's an understandable thought pattern: you worked hard,

you deserve this. But for many founders, lifestyle inflation becomes a substitute for purpose. When the void hits, they try to fill it with stuff.

Or they turn hobbies into obsessions. Take golf – I've watched founders throw themselves into it like it's their new business. They're at the club every day, playing with expensive coaches, buying the latest equipment, joining exclusive courses. What used to bring them weekend joy becomes their full-time identity. But there's often something missing: most of their mates still need to go to the office. So they're out there playing alone, wondering why something that used to be fun now feels empty. Or is done with strangers.

Some founders go even further, treating relationships like acquisitions. As Warren Buffett supposedly said, "Many of my mates later in life decide to go and get a trophy wife, but if you ask me, it's just the booby prize." It's another form of hedonic adaptation – seeking external validation through status symbols rather than doing the internal work.

The real danger is when one addiction (workaholism anyone?) simply transforms into another. Elton John famously spent £40 million in under two years after getting clean from drugs and alcohol, including £293,000 just on flowers. He'd conquered cocaine and alcohol, but the addictive pattern remained – it just found a new outlet. "I can't have one pair of shoes, I can't have one CD, I can't have one bunch of flowers, one car, one ornament," he later admitted.

This pattern strips the joy out of everything it touches, turning pleasures into compulsions and relationships into transactions. But even those who resist the lure of lifestyle inflation often fall into a different trap.

WAIT UNTIL YOU GET BORED

Perhaps the most seductive pattern: founders who jump back into building something new, not because they've found their calling, but because they can't handle the stillness.

. . . .

I watched this almost happen to Aaron. He was referred to me by a mutual close friend, Harry – a skilled board director and chair. He was concerned that Aaron was flirting with burnout and addicted to the build, chasing the rush of foundership.

Aaron had just closed the sale of his software company – a solid eight-figure exit that set him up for life. We met for coffee three weeks after the wire hit his account, and he was buzzing with excitement about his next venture.

"I'm already incorporating the new company," he told me. "I've got this idea for a marketplace platform, and I want to move fast before someone else builds it."

I stopped him. "Aaron, can I share something with you? Wait until you get bored."

He looked at me like I'd suggested he burn money. "Bored? I can't afford to get bored. The market won't wait."

"The market will always be there. But this moment – this space between who you were and who you'll become – this won't. You'll never get this chance again to actually figure out who you are, versus what you think you should build."

I told him about my own experience with my third startup, Ambit. How even when I didn't need the money, even when I'd already proven I could build and exit successfully, I got caught up in the mayhem instead of the meaning. How I'd confused movement with progress, busyness with purpose. (I'll come back to that story later in the book – it taught me everything about what makes an exit truly successful.)

"Give yourself six months," I said. "Do the personal projects you've been putting off. Idle around the house. Travel without checking emails. Spend quality family time. And wait. Wait until you're genuinely, deeply bored. That's when you'll know you're ready to build something again – but from choice, not from discomfort."

Aaron spent the next six months doing exactly that. He renovated his garage workshop, took a photography course, read books that had nothing to do with business. He travelled to places he'd always wanted to see but never had time for. He had long conversations with his wife about what they actually wanted their life to look like. When I saw him again, he looked different. Calmer. More grounded.

"That was the best advice anyone's ever given me," he said. "I thought I was ready to start something new, but I was just running from the void. When I finally got bored – really, genuinely bored – I knew I was ready. And the business I'm building now is completely different from what I was rushing into. It's something I actually care about, not just something to keep me busy."

The difference between premature re-entry and genuine readiness isn't timeline – it's motivation. Are you building because you can't sit with stillness, or because you've found something that genuinely calls to you? The founders who wait until they're bored usually build something far more meaningful than those who rush back in to escape the void. But even those who avoid premature re-entry often fall into the final trap.

BORROWED IDENTITIES

The fourth pattern is perhaps the most subtle: founders who try to solve their identity crisis by immediately adopting new roles and titles, without doing the internal work to understand what they actually want to contribute.

The Board Member Collector joins multiple boards simply to recreate the feeling of being important and needed. They're attracted to the status and the familiar rhythm of meetings and decisions, but often lack genuine passion for the specific companies or causes they're endeavouring to serve.

The Instant Philanthropist – I've done this one myself. You start a foundation or dive into charitable work not because you've found your cause, but because successful people are supposed to give back. It's performative generosity, and in my case, I was doing a startup all over again!

The Advisor/Mentor Circuit takes on multiple advisory roles and mentoring relationships, filling their calendar with coffee meetings and strategic sessions. They love feeling needed again, but lacking focus, they often end up giving generic advice to founders who don't particularly value it.

The common thread? Rushing to fill the identity void with external validation rather than doing the uncomfortable work of figuring out who you actually want to become. Here's what I've learned: these four patterns are all attempts to avoid the same thing. **The space between who you were as a founder and who you're meant to become next.** What David Brooks calls your "Second Mountain" – the meaningful work that comes after financial success – can't be rushed or performed. It has to be discovered. But first, you have to be willing to sit in the uncertainty long enough to find it.

I'll show you how to find and climb yours in Chapter 16.

THE MENTAL PREP YOU NEED

Your business has been the scaffolding for your identity: providing structure, validation, community, purpose, and challenge. When you sell, that scaffolding is removed, revealing whatever foundation exists beneath it. That's why the post-exit crash feels so physical, so visceral.

The smartest founders I've worked with approach this transition deliberately. In an ideal world, this work happens before the wire hits, but most of us are too consumed with the exit process to think beyond the closing. The key is starting this reflection as soon as you can:

- Who will I be without this company?
- What's the mission behind the money?
- What will give me purpose once the novelty wears off?
- Can I sit in the stillness without immediately building again?

If you don't define your next chapter, the void will do it for you – usually through one of those four patterns we just explored.

Look, I won't sugarcoat it – standing on that shore watching your ship sail away feels like hell. I've been there, staring at my bank account with enough zeros to last a lifetime and still feeling completely empty inside.

What nobody prepared me for: that identity void isn't a bug in the system, it's a feature. It's supposed to hurt. That discomfort isn't just pain; it's the sensation of your cocoon breaking open.

My friend Jazz called me three months after selling her marketing agency for eight figures. "I'm rich and miserable," she laughed, but it wasn't really a laugh. "I thought I'd feel free. Instead, I feel useless."

Six months later, that same Jazz was building something completely different – not another business (yet), but a frame-work for her life that aligned with who she actually was, not just who she'd been pretending to be for 12 years as "Founder Jazz".

"The emptiness forced me to dig deeper," she told me over drinks. "Without it, I'd have just recreated the same stress patterns in a new logo."

That's what this journey is actually about. Not escaping the discomfort, but moving through it with *intention*. Not running from the void, but using it as fertile ground to plant something authentic. Every founder I know who genuinely thrived after their exit used this transition as rocket fuel for their most meaningful work. And with the right approach, so can you.

But first, we need to understand why so many founders who "win" the exit game still feel like they've lost something essential. In the next chapter, we'll explore why most exits don't feel like freedom – and what you can do **to ensure yours does.**

✔ CHECKPOINT: WHO ARE YOU AFTER THIS?

Here's your pre-sale diagnostic. Be brutally honest.

- What scares you about no longer being "the founder"?
- If I handed you $10 million tomorrow, what would you do with your time?
- If you couldn't start another business for a year, how would you stay grounded?
- Who do you want to become – now that you no longer have to prove yourself?

If you don't know the answers, that's okay. But it means your work isn't done yet. Not in the business; in you.

CHAPTER 3

The Tyranny of Drive

"No man is free who is not master of himself."

– Epictetus

If money isn't the answer – what is?

Founders don't simply want freedom. They want **relief.**

Relief from pressure. Relief from responsibility. Relief from the constant weight of management. In the darkest moments of building, the exit gleams like an escape hatch – a way out of the cage they've inadvertently built around themselves.

But relief is only temporary. **Freedom is structural.**

Relief comes from removing an immediate source of pain. Freedom comes from creating conditions that align with your authentic needs and values. Relief requires nothing of you but escape. Freedom demands something much harder: self-awareness and intentional design.

. . . .

In 2007, Clark Benson sold his company, eCrush, for $14 million. After grinding nonstop for 12 years, you'd expect he'd take a moment to breathe, celebrate, reflect – maybe even disappear for a bit.

But he didn't.

Instead, Clark immediately jumped into building Ranker, his next venture. He later admitted this was a mistake. No reflection, no clarity – just a new logo, a new company, and (as it turned out) the exact same struggles.

Long hours, constant pressure, operational headaches – everything he thought he had left behind. The issues followed him because he never paused to understand why he was really exiting in the first place.

Clark was trapped in what I call the "Look-Alike Company" cycle – rebuilding familiar problems because freedom wasn't something he'd intentionally designed.

Eventually, Clark got clear. Ranker turned around dramatically, becoming a powerhouse with over $50 million in annual revenue, strategic acquisitions, and millions of monthly users. But getting there was harder – and more painful – than it needed to be.

Clark's story highlights a common founder myth: that an exit, money, or stepping away automatically means freedom and inner harmony. Without clear intention, we just recreate the same patterns again and again.

Freedom isn't automatic.

Freedom needs to be **deliberately designed.**

If you don't pause to reflect and reset before your next chapter, you'll simply live the last one again.

The bad news is that this is a hard truth to face up to, and can be tricky to navigate. The good news is you're aware this is coming. And, as you know as an entrepreneur, growth exists on the other side of something hard.

*A common founder myth: an
exit, money, or stepping away
automatically means freedom
and fulfillment. Without clear
intention, we just recreate the
same patterns again and again.*

SUCCESS ≠ REST

People see your success and think you're lucky. What they don't see is the monkey on your back; the one with the tiny whip that never lets you rest.

I call it the **Tyranny of Drive.**

It's that voice in your head at 4:30 AM saying, "Get up, there's work to be done!" while your body begs for one more hour of sleep. It's checking email before your feet hit the floor. It's the inability to watch a movie without thinking about your business.

Drive is a gift and a curse. It built my first company. It destroyed my first marriage.

"You're so motivated," people tell me with admiration in their voice. What they don't understand is that motivation implies choice. This doesn't feel like a choice. It feels like being possessed.

I suspect you've felt this?

It's why we have this thing called **founder burnout.**

According to research by Sifted, Startup Snapshot and b2venture[1], it afflicts over 50% of founders. 94% have experienced mental health issues. One in two of you is on the brink of your work killing you.

Society celebrates drive. Hustle culture glorifies it.

"Rise and grind."
"Sleep when you're dead."

We paint it as the hero of the success story.

But there's a dark side no one talks about: drive doesn't know when to quit. It doesn't understand vacations, weekends, or "enough". It's a brilliant engine without an off switch.

Those without it envy those who have it. Those afflicted by it envy people who can simply... rest.

I've seen this tyranny play out in three distinct ways:

1. The Satisfaction Mirage: No achievement ever feels like enough. You hit your goal, and instead of celebration, your brain immediately moves the target. $10 million becomes "but what about $100 million?" Success becomes a horizon that continually recedes as you approach it.

2. The Identity Merger: Your drive becomes who you are, not just what you do. When someone asks, "Who are you?" without your company or achievements, you draw a blank. This becomes devastatingly apparent after an exit.

3. The Rest Resistance: You literally forget how to relax. Downtime creates anxiety. Vacation feels like withdrawal. Your nervous system has forgotten how to operate in any gear besides fifth.

A founder I worked with – a brilliant woman who built a $70 million business – told me:

"I used to think drive was this gift that made me special. Now I realise it's like being a fantastic racehorse who doesn't know how to stand still without bucking. Sometimes I just want to graze in a field, but I've forgotten how."

Learning to master drive rather than be mastered by it might be the most important skill nobody teaches entrepreneurs.

Drive isn't bad. It's just untamed. In 2004, I founded my first company, Potentia – a reinvention of the resourcing model, blending leadership coaching with executive search. Early growth was slow as the model took hold, but by year two we were in a stratospheric rise, winning multiple local and international entrepreneurship and growth awards. Ultimately, we landed in the IT Services category with a stable of offerings centred on people solutions.

After just over a decade, despite the accolades and growth, fulfilment was fading and I was burning out. The very drive that fuelled the business had become my challenge. It was relentless and, in hindsight, untamed.

By 2015, after a difficult period of self-reflection, I decided it was time to sell. I chose to hand over stewardship to my senior team (A Succession Exit – more on this later), trusting them to grow the business from $25 million to over three times that size today.

Drive isn't bad. It's just untamed. Like fire, it can warm your

You must consciously build a structure around clarity and purpose – otherwise you'll just recreate old patterns.

home or burn it down. The founders who survive long-term aren't the ones with the most drive - they're the ones who've learned to harness it, direct it, and yes, occasionally turn it off.

After my first exit, I didn't realize how much I'd been running on adrenaline and cortisol for years. My body literally didn't know how to function without that chemical cocktail. The crash was physical as well as emotional.

Mastering drive—rather than being mastered by it—may be the most important skill no one teaches entrepreneurs.

It takes:

- Building identity beyond achievement
- Creating concrete boundaries that protect rest

- Developing metrics for life, not just business
- Learning to value being, not just doing

The work doesn't end when the money hits your account. It's just beginning. The hardest challenge isn't building the business; it's rebuilding yourself into someone who knows how to live without the whip.

I learned this the hard way. I assumed money and time meant freedom, but really, they created space to confront myself - something I hadn't planned on. Without purpose and structure, I found myself solving the same old problems because I didn't know who I was without them.

You must consciously build a structure around clarity and purpose - or you'll end up recreating old patterns.

CONSTRAINTS

Real freedom isn't the absence of constraints. It's the presence of the right constraints – ones aligned with your authentic needs, values, and strengths.

Rory understood this when planning his exit. Unlike the bulk of founders who focus exclusively on valuation and terms, Rory spent equal time designing his post-exit life.

"I realised I didn't want an empty calendar," he told me. "I wanted a calendar filled with the right things."

Rory's approach to structural freedom involved four elements:

1. Value-Based Decision Architecture

Before his exit, Rory identified his core values and created explicit decision filters for post-exit opportunities. When a prestigious board seat came his way that violated these filters, he declined – despite the status it would have conferred.

2. Relationship Restructuring

Rory proactively rebuilt key relationships around shared interests rather than business roles. This prevented the common post-exit experience of relationship voids when professional contexts disappear.

3. Purpose Continuity

Rather than seeing his exit as the end of his purpose, Rory identified the underlying impact that had always motivated him – separate from the specific business – and designed ways to continue that impact in new contexts.

4. Moderated Optionality

Contrary to conventional wisdom that "more options equals more freedom", Rory intentionally limited his post-exit options to prevent decision paralysis and maintain focus on his priority areas.

The result wasn't the empty freedom of permanent vacation (which few founders want anyway). It was the aligned freedom of a life designed around his authentic drivers rather than reactive patterns.

Four years after his exit, Rory hasn't started another company. Not because he couldn't, but because he doesn't need to. He's found structural freedom – the kind that doesn't depend on which business he's running or whether he's running one at all.

*True freedom begins with
recognising attachments
and loosening their hold on your
sense of self – ideally before
your exit, not after.*

ANCIENT WISDOM FOR MODERN FOUNDERS

The challenge of true freedom isn't unique to modern entrepreneurs. Philosophers have wrestled with these questions for millennia, and their insights offer powerful guidance for founders approaching exits.

The Stoics understood that external circumstances (even wealth) cannot deliver genuine freedom.

Epictetus said:

> *"Make the best use of what is in your power,
> and take the rest as it happens."*

Buddhist philosophy echoes this through the concept of attachment: freedom comes not from getting what you want, but from breaking the belief that specific outcomes are required for your worth and happiness.

True freedom begins with recognising attachments and loosening their hold on your sense of self – ideally before your exit, not after.

WHAT FREEDOM ACTUALLY REQUIRES

Through my work in steering hundreds of founders through their exits, I've noticed that genuine freedom always comes down to three things: **clarity, agency,** and **structure.**

Clarity means knowing yourself deeply – your authentic values, strengths, and what drives you when no one's watching. Not the founder version of you, but the real you underneath.

Agency is about genuine choice. Not just having options, but having the internal capacity to choose consciously rather than just react out of habit or fear.

Structure means intentionally designing conditions that support who you truly are, rather than defaulting to familiar patterns that worked for someone else's life.

What I believe now: **you need all three.** Clarity without agency leaves you knowing what you want but unable to choose it. Agency without structure gives you the power to choose but no framework to sustain those choices. Structure without clarity just builds a beautiful cage around the wrong life.

The deal can make you wealthy.
Only clarity can make you free.

"SO... WHAT ARE YOU GOING TO DO NEXT?"

In my part of the world, most people are too polite to ask how much money the sale netted. So the very first question you'll likely hear from your friends and family is a derivative of:

"What's next?"

There's so much expectation sitting behind this otherwise harmless and well-meaning question. The intention may indeed just be curiosity and care, but it nearly always manifests as pressure: "the world expects something even greater from me now" kind of thing.

I've framed this as being akin to an avid sports fan: the enquirer wants to observe another amazing death-defying feat from you. They may even be living vicariously. Either way, I'd strongly suggest a simple "I'm going to take time out and see what arises" approach. It defuses the question respectfully and quickly. And authorises your lizard brain to take a break.

We'll talk more about this across Part IV.

Remember: your exit is *not the end of your story*. It's a plot point. Whether it becomes a positive turning point or just another loop in the same cycle depends not on the deal terms, but on your willingness to see yourself clearly.

Freedom isn't a given. Freedom is an inside job – and a structural one. Design your future now, or you'll live your past again.

✔ FINAL CHECKPOINT FOR PART I:
ARE YOU SEEKING RELIEF OR FREEDOM?

Here's your freedom diagnostic. Be brutally honest.

- What are you trying to escape by selling? (Pressure? Responsibility? The feeling of being trapped?)
- When you imagine your post-exit life, do you see empty time or purposeful time?
- What drives you besides money and validation? (If you can't answer this, you're not ready for freedom)
- How will you know when you're truly free vs. just relieved?

If you can't answer these questions clearly, your freedom isn't fully designed yet. And if they make you uncomfortable, that's the point. Without design, history repeats itself – just with more money in your pocket.

PART II

The Value Dimension

SEEING VALUE THROUGH THE BUYER'S EYES

You're not a conventional founder.
Why use conventional metrics?

CHAPTER 4

The Great Valuation Myth

> *"Price is what you pay. Value is what you get."*
>
> – Warren Buffett

What assumptions have you made about how your business would be valued – and where did those beliefs come from?

. . . .

By mid-2009, the GFC was in full swing. Iconic banks were hitting the wall; bankruptcy, fraud and criminal proceedings were on everyone's minds. The financial world was in ashes.

Then Disney writes a $4 billion cheque for Marvel Entertainment – a company bringing in just $500 million annually.

That's an 8× revenue multiple during economic collapse, in an industry where 4× was considered generous in good times.

"Bob Iger has lost his mind," the pundits said.

Fast-forward: that "over-priced" acquisition has generated *over $28 billion in box office alone. Add merchandise, theme parks and streaming, and the ROI becomes comical. This wasn't spreadsheet math. It was possibility math.*

Extraordinary multiples aren't about current worth; they're about what problem you solve in the acquirer's future.

Disney didn't buy Marvel for 2009. They bought it for what it would become: the key to younger demographics and decades of content potential.

....

This wasn't spreadsheet math.
It was possibility math.

....

Serial acquirers make similar bets, buying:

- Time (market entry years faster)
- Talent (impossible to assemble teams)
- Technology (competitive moats)
- Trajectory (removing threats or securing growth)

What buy-side M&A teams don't want you to know: revenue multiples are often the **least imaginative language of value.** Extraordinary exits happen when you create businesses that solve strategic problems worth far more than what shows on a P&L.

Build something that becomes key in someone else's future, and the multiple follows. Just ask Disney shareholders about that "over-priced" Marvel deal now.

Your business doesn't need to be a cultural empire to command strategic value. But it does need to solve a future problem for someone bigger than you.

The most successful founders think like cartographers, not map collectors.

THE MAP IS NOT THE TERRITORY: WHEN VALUE DEFIES VALUATION

Ever held a map and thought, "This doesn't match what I'm seeing"? Maps simplify: mountains become contour lines, rivers thin blue threads. They're useful guides but incomplete representations.

The phrase "the map is not the territory" – coined by Polish-American philosopher and engineer Alfred Korzybski – reminds us that models of reality aren't reality itself. **Our abstractions, formulas and frameworks are tools, not truth.**

In business, this distinction is critical. Valuation metrics are maps. They simplify the complex reality of business value into digestible formulas like "9× revenue" or "7× EBITDA". These maps offer orientation, but miss the terrain's richness.

The most expensive mistakes and the greatest opportunities live in the gap between map and territory. The most successful founders think like cartographers, not map collectors.

Your job is to create territory so valuable that **acquirers will discard those maps entirely.**

Valuation is psychology, not maths

At the end of every first meeting I have with a founder, we inevitably land on the topic of company valuation. Almost without fail, I get one of two reactions: either a number that's absurdly high or one that's shockingly low.

Most founders carry a simple mental model of valuation:

> **Revenue (or EBITDA) × Industry Multiple**
> **= Company Value**

It's understandable. They scan exit news, swap stories with peers, and hunt for "the multiple" that applies to their sector. Then they do the math and land on *their number*.

It feels logical. But it's dangerously incomplete.

Valuation isn't math. **It's psychology.** It's a story buyers tell themselves about what your business could be – *in their hands.* That story is shaped by perception, not just performance.

Yet founders consistently fall into three traps that distort their valuation expectations:

The Past-Anchor Trap: Founders unconsciously attach value to the sacrifices they've made – the years of grind, capital invested, weekends missed. This is essentially sunk cost. The past is pride; valuation is about potential.

The Comparison Trap: Seeing a competitor's exit headline, founders assume they're worth more without understanding

Your business isn't worth what it cost to build. It's worth what it's worth to someone else.

the buyer's motives, deal terms, or timing. Strategic value isn't visible from the outside. Comparing deals without context leads to false benchmarks and inflated expectations.

The Projection Trap: Many founders pitch a valuation based on where the company could go, *if* everything goes right. But buyers price based on where you are now, plus what *they* believe they can do with it. That delta belongs to them, not you.

These traps create a credibility gap that can stall deals, sour negotiations, or leave millions on the table.

Your business isn't worth what it cost to build. It's worth what it's worth to someone else.

VALUATION VS. TERMS: THE HIDDEN REALITY

Here's another trap founders fall into: obsessing about headline valuation while ignoring deal terms.

Consider two offers:

- Offer A: $15 million valuation, but half tied to tough earn-outs, and you stay locked in operationally for three years.

- Offer B: $10 million cash up-front, quick exit, minimal constraints.

Founders, especially first-time sellers, typically gravitate to the bigger number. But the smarter play is often the lower valuation with better terms. **Terms create freedom,** structure, and clarity – or frustration, restriction, and regret.

You never bank the headline valuation. You bank the terms.

You never bank the headline valuation. You bank the terms.

WHAT BUYERS ACTUALLY PAY FOR

In hundreds of exit discussions, founders focus on what they've built, while buyers focus on what they're *buying*. These are **not the same thing.**

When sophisticated buyers evaluate your business, they're asking four questions you probably aren't:

1. Strategic fit – how does this amplify my strategy?

The highest valuations don't come from buyers who want what you've built. They come from buyers who need what you've built to fulfil their strategic objectives.

Consider Walmart's seemingly insane $3.3 billion acquisition of Jet.com in 2016 – a company with just $1 billion in revenue and exactly zero profits. Walmart wasn't buying spreadsheets; they were buying survival. Facing digital extinction at Amazon's hands, Walmart paid that premium not for what Jet.com was, but for what Walmart wasn't – digitally fluent, algorithmically sophisticated, and connected to urban millennials who viewed Walmart with the enthusiasm usually reserved for dental surgery. Walmart wasn't buying a business; they were buying a lifeline.

2. Risk profile – how much risk am I taking?

Buyers need confidence in future performance. Every element that threatens that confidence – customer concentration, team dependencies, competitive threats, technology debt – directly impacts valuation.

A business with $2 million in EBITDA and distributed risk (diversified customer base, strong team, documented processes) will often sell for more than a business with $3 million in EBITDA but concentrated risk (one key customer, founder-dependent operations).

3. Integration speed – how quickly can I extract value?

Speed is currency in acquisitions. Buyers pay premiums for businesses they can quickly integrate, cross-sell to existing customers, or use to block competitive threats.

I watched a midsize company acquire a smaller competitor for 3x the "market rate" simply because the target company had already built integrations with enterprise platforms the acquirer was targeting. The speed advantage was worth millions.

4. Founder readiness – is the founder an asset or liability?

The way you show up in the sale process – your energy, clarity, and detachment – directly impacts valuation. Buyers are constantly evaluating: "Will this founder help or hinder the transition?" Your demeanour becomes part of your value.

A founder who demonstrates emotional maturity, clear vision for post-acquisition success, and appropriate detachment can increase valuation by 20% or more through buyer confidence alone.

Remember: buyers don't pay for what you've built. They pay for what it becomes in their hands. Make that vision undeniable.

YOUR BUSINESS, THEIR VISION

If you take nothing else from this chapter, take this:

Value is subjective.

The same business can have wildly different valuations depending on the buyer. A private equity firm might see you as worth 4–5x EBITDA – predictable, safe, straightforward. A strategic buyer, however, might see 10x–15x if you unlock distribution, remove a competitor, or speed their market entry.

Your job is to identify and court the buyers who see maximum strategic value then position yourself to **amplify it.**

The most successful exits occur when founders make the mental shift from "What is my business worth based on what

I've built?" to "What is my business worth to this specific buyer, given their strategic objectives?"

Remember: buyers don't pay for what you've built. They pay for what it becomes in their hands. Make that vision undeniable.

In Chapter 6, I cover in detail how to make yourself irresistible to buyers – the specific strategies that transform you from just another acquisition target into the company they can't afford to lose.

✔ **CHECKPOINT:** WHAT'S YOUR BUSINESS REALLY WORTH?

- Can you clearly articulate why your business is strategically valuable to a specific buyer (beyond revenue and profit)?
- What risks will a buyer perceive in your company and how will you proactively address them?
- Have you emotionally inflated your valuation? And how would you know if you did?
- Are you thinking about valuation alone or terms, structure, and strategic leverage?

CHAPTER 5

The Buyer's Mind

*How acquirers think, what they fear,
and what they really want.*

*"The most valuable thing you can do in negotiation
is deeply understand the other side's fears."*

– Chris Voss, author of Never Split the Difference

Are you positioning around what you've built, or what they need?

In the last chapter, we explored the myths around business valuation – how founders often rely on simple formulas, while buyers make psychological decisions rooted in strategic fit and risk perception.

Understanding valuation is only half the equation, though.

To sell your business well, you can't just *look* valuable. You need to understand what the buyer actually *wants* – and, more importantly, what keeps them up at night.

Buyers don't think like you do. You've spent years obsessing over growth, cash-flow, culture, and customers. Buyers? They're wondering if your business is a landmine wrapped in a pretty pitch deck.

> They're thinking:
>
> "What's broken here that I can't see yet?"
>
> "Will this thing actually work when we own it?"
>
> "Is this founder going to be a total nightmare post-deal?"

The best exits don't come from pitching harder. They come from understanding what drives your buyer's decisions.

Founders who land the biggest wins are the ones who **stop thinking like founders, and start thinking like buyers.** Not forever. Just long enough to see your business the way they do.

That's what this chapter is about.

We're going to crack open the psychology of buyers. Their motivations. Their fears. The quiet stuff that shapes decisions but rarely shows up in a term sheet. And we'll introduce a tool that helps make sense of it all:

The Buyer Motivation Matrix™

Once you see where your buyer is coming from – and what they're really buying – you'll understand how to position your business in a way they can't ignore.

Let's get inside their heads.

INSIDE THE BUYER'S MINDSET

Every buyer I've ever met walks into the room with one thought hammering in their brain:

"What's wrong with this business?"

Not "how exciting", not "what's the upside?" Their default setting is suspicion – and they're right to be paranoid.

Think about it. When you've bought anything significant – a house, a car, definitely a company – your real anxiety isn't what you know. It's the land mines you can't see. The stuff lurking beneath the surface that might blow up in your face after you've written the cheque.

Buyers who ignore this scepticism pay dearly for it.

Just ask Hewlett-Packard (HP), who in 2011 dropped a staggering **$11.1 billion** on UK software company Autonomy. On paper, it looked perfect: growing revenue, strong IP, strategic fit. They saw a unicorn.

What they missed – or ignored – was the financial sleight-of-hand. Autonomy had been dressing up low-margin hardware sales as premium software revenue. A clever accounting trick. An $8.8 billion problem.

HP eventually wrote down 80% of the purchase price and spent the next decade drowning in lawsuits and blame-shifting.

The issue wasn't just fraud. It was **blind optimism.** They fell in love with the story and forgot to check under the hood.

This is why today's buyers approach you like you're selling a used car with fresh paint. They've been burned before. They've watched beautiful pitch decks crumble during due diligence. They've paid premium prices for businesses with terminal illnesses.

So when they meet you, they're not thinking, "This could transform our business." They're thinking, **"Where's the hidden catch?"**

Your job isn't to sell harder. It's to make that voice go quiet – not with spin, but with **transparency.**

Walk in already answering the questions they haven't even asked yet.

Remember this:
not all goals are financial.

Try this for framing:

Buyers don't fall in love with what you've built. They fall in love with what it can become once it's theirs – if it's structurally sound, clean, and strategically aligned.

ENTER: THE BUYER MOTIVATION MATRIX™

If you want to understand what drives buyers, don't start with spreadsheets. Start with **psychology.**

We make the mistake of thinking the acquirer is just "The Corporation". But behind every deal, there's a person making a bet – a bet that buying your business will move them closer to their goals and further from their risks.

Remember this: not all goals are financial.

Some buyers want control. Some want speed. Some want glory.

Some just want to beat the other guy to the punch.

In my experience, the most dangerous thing a founder can do is assume that _every_ buyer is wired the same way. They're not. You wouldn't sell a Ferrari the same way you'd sell a Toyota. And you sure as hell wouldn't sell a warhorse the same way you'd sell a Trojan one.

That's why I built this: **The Buyer Motivation Matrix™.** A simple way to map out who you're dealing with, and what really matters to them.

Here's how it maps out across motivations and priorities:

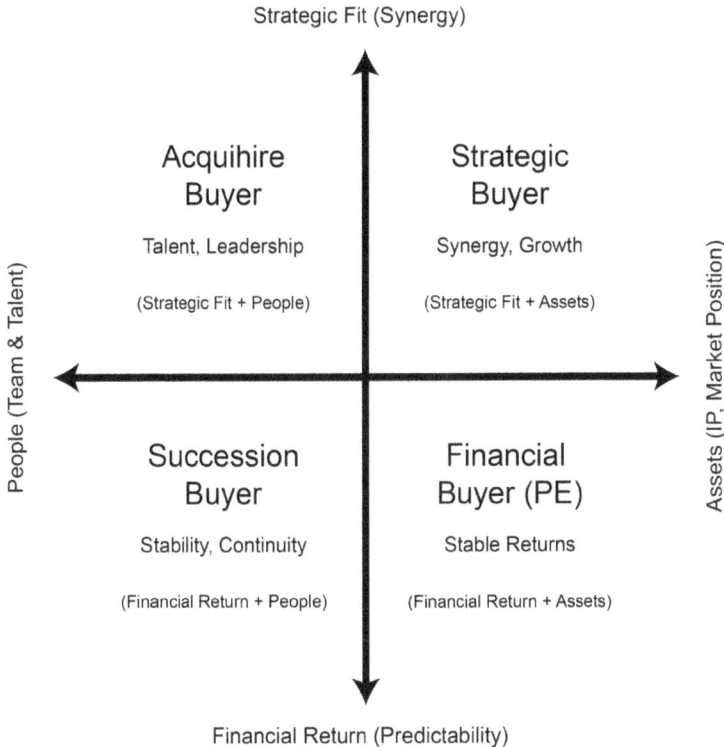

Strategic Fit (Synergy)

Acquihire Buyer	**Strategic Buyer**
Talent, Leadership	Synergy, Growth
(Strategic Fit + People)	(Strategic Fit + Assets)
Succession Buyer	**Financial Buyer (PE)**
Stability, Continuity	Stable Returns
(Financial Return + People)	(Financial Return + Assets)

People (Team & Talent) — Assets (IP, Market Position)

Financial Return (Predictability)

THE FIVE BUYER ARCHETYPES

Strategic Buyers (Strategic Fit + Assets)

These are the big players looking to level up, and fast. They want synergy, market share, distribution, and defensibility. If your product, IP, or customer base gives them a competitive edge, they'll lean in hard.

They ask: "Does this help us win our next five years?"

Think: Google buying YouTube, Disney buying Marvel.

> **How to identify them:** They're usually large companies in your industry or adjacent sectors. They talk about "strategic fit", "synergies" and "market positioning". They ask detailed questions about your customer base, technology, and competitive advantages.

De-risking it for them: Focus on integration clarity and strategic narrative.

Financial Buyers (Financial Return + Assets)

Private equity firms, family offices, and other investors in this category are buying stability. They want strong cashflow, clean operations, and a path to consistent ROI. Growth is nice. *Predictability is essential.*

They ask: "Can we count on this thing to keep throwing off cash?"

Think: A PE firm buying a profitable SaaS business with low churn and high margins.

> **How to identify them:** They lead with financial metrics in conversations. They want to see your EBITDA, cash flow statements, and growth projections. They ask about operational efficiency and scalability potential.

De-risking it for them: Emphasise financial transparency and operational efficiency

Acquihire Buyers (Strategic Fit + People)

These buyers aren't really after your product. They're after your **team**. Talent is hard to build from scratch, and if you've assembled a high-performance crew, you've built something valuable even if the product never scales.

They ask: "Can this team accelerate what we're already building?"

Think: Facebook buying smaller startups just to onboard engineers.

> **How to identify them:** They spend more time talking to your team than analysing your financials. They ask about retention, team dynamics, and individual skill sets. They often come from tech companies facing talent shortages, plus high-impact professional services teams for power move market plays.

De-risking it for them: Show employment surveys, influencer currency and retention strategies.

Succession Buyers (Financial Return + People)

Often overlooked, these are the buyers who want a solid team and a steady ship. This could be a management buyout, a search fund, or a family office looking for long-term value. They care about continuity and operational maturity.

They ask: "Will this keep running – and growing – without drama?"

Think: A search fund buying out a well-run services business with stable leadership.

> **How to identify them:** They focus heavily on leadership depth and operational systems. They ask about your management team's capabilities and succession planning. They want to understand day-to-day operations in detail.

De-risking it for them: Prove founder redundancy, business independence and leadership depth.

Competitive Buyers (Across multiple quadrants)

These are the "chess move" acquirers. They might care about your assets, your people, your tech – or just keeping you out of a rival's hands. Their motivations can be opportunistic, aggressive, or purely defensive.

They ask: "Does buying this remove a threat–or give us leverage?"

Think: Uber buying a regional ride-share competitor.

> **How to identify them:** They're usually direct competitors or companies in your supply chain. They may approach quickly with aggressive offers. They ask strategic questions about your market position and competitive threats.

WHY THE MATRIX MATTERS

When you know which quadrant your buyer is operating from, everything gets clearer:

- emphasise *integration speed* for strategics
- emphasise *EBITDA cleanliness* for financials
- emphasise *team calibre* for acquihires
- emphasise *stability* for succession buyers
- emphasise *competitive threat* for rivals

Each one sees your business through a different lens – and **they pay for different things.**

This matrix helps you get ahead of their questions, their

goals, and their concerns, so you can walk in already speaking their language. Buyers pay more for businesses that feel familiar. This matrix helps you become **the one they've been hoping to find**.

HOW TO SPEAK EACH BUYER'S LANGUAGE

Once you know which type of buyer you're dealing with, you can finally stop talking about yourself and start talking about what they care about:

> **Strategic Buyer:** "How does this make us faster, stronger, harder to beat?"
>
> **Financial Buyer:** "Will this throw off cash without surprises?"
>
> **Acquihire Buyer:** "Can this team solve our problems tomorrow?"
>
> **Succession Buyer:** "Can I sleep at night after closing?"
>
> **Competitive Buyer:** "What's the cost of not buying?"

Strategic Buyers want to know: "How does this make us faster, stronger, or harder to beat?" Don't bore them with your growth story – show them how you plug the holes in their strategy. They're buying speed and competitive advantage, not your revenue chart.

Financial Buyers want to know: "Will this thing print money reliably?" Skip the vision speech. Show them clean numbers, predictable cash flow, and a business that runs without drama. They're buying a money machine, not your passion project.

Acquihire Buyers want to know: "Can this team actually solve our problems?" Forget the product demo –- put your best

The key?
Stop selling what you built.
Start selling what they need.

people in front of them. Show retention rates, team chemistry, social influencer currency and why these specific humans are impossible to replace. They're buying talent, not technology.

Succession Buyers want to know: "Can I sleep at night after buying this?" They want to see a business that runs itself, with leaders who know what they're doing and systems that work without you. They're buying peace of mind, not a fixer-upper.

Competitive Buyers want to know: "What happens if I don't buy this?" Create urgency without being pushy. Show them what their world looks like if a competitor gets you instead. They're buying strategic defence, not just strategic offence.

The key? Stop selling what you built. Start selling what they need.

✔ CHECKPOINT: BUYER PERSPECTIVE DIAGNOSTIC

Ask yourself:

- Which buyer archetype sees maximum value in your business?
- Can you articulate your strategic value to each type?
- Are you positioning around what you've built, or what they need?
- Have you listed specific companies in each category that might buy you?

If your answers aren't clear, your positioning isn't either.

But now, you have my tool – **the Buyer Motivation Matrix™** – to align your story precisely with your buyer's motivations.

Start thinking like a buyer, even if you're not thinking of exiting yet. Start now.

Because buyers buy clarity, not noise and guesswork – and pay a premium for it.

"A decision is a risk rooted in the courage of being free."

– Paul Tillich

*"Fear is interest paid in advance
on a debt you may never owe."*

– Mark Twain

CHAPTER 6

Make Yourself Irresistible

"People don't buy goods and services. They buy relations, stories, and magic."

– Seth Godin

"The art of persuasion is not to impose logic, but to arouse longing."

– Antoine de Saint-Exupéry

Can you master the art of becoming the acquisition your buyer can't walk away from?

I've got a thing for trainers. Not in that obsessive "stockpile pristine Jordans in their boxes" way, but in the everyday sense of "damn, these things look good." About twenty-five pairs; modest enough not to be ridiculous, but enough to make the choice each morning interesting.

When I was younger, it was easy – Adidas Superstars, Nike Airs. They were cool, affordable, and everywhere. Then life changed. A bit more cash, a bit more taste (taste IS subjective; not everyone loves my neon yellow Diesels). Suddenly, I'm wearing Gucci. Louis Vuitton. Sneakers that are priced at more than an international flight.

Are they more comfortable? Not really.

But that's not why you buy Gucci or LV trainers.

You buy the story. You buy what it says about you, how it makes you feel, what it signals to the world.

And that's exactly how buyers think when they're looking at your business.

They're not just buying what it is.

They're buying what it represents – to them, their team, their board, and their future.

WHEN MULTIPLES BREAK MATH: FACEBOOK'S WHATSAPP GAMBLE

In 2014, Facebook dropped $19 billion on WhatsApp. Technically $21 billion after stock adjustments – but when you're swinging the biggest acquisition bat in tech history, what's another couple billion?

WhatsApp had $20 million in revenue. That's a 950× revenue multiple. Not a typo.

Let that sink in:

55 employees → $345 million per head

450 million users → $42 per user

Revenue model that barely qualified as one

Wall Street lost its collective mind. "Zuckerberg's gone insane!" "This isn't M&A – it's a donation!"

But they were reading the map, not seeing the territory.

The deal wasn't about revenue. It was about existential defence and exponential growth.

WhatsApp was exploding faster than anything Facebook had encountered. It had become the communication backbone

> *Transformative deals don't go to the highest bidder. They go to the clearest story. The fastest mover. The buyer who makes the founder feel like the match is inevitable.*

in massive markets like India and Brazil. And critically, it was mobile-native when Facebook was still awkwardly adapting to the smartphone revolution.

And here's what everyone missed: this deal was competitive as hell.

Google was hovering with a fatter chequebook. But Zuck didn't win by outbidding – he won by aligning. He pitched a shared vision, not just a bigger number; making this a dual-narrative story.

"The most important thing," he said, "was aligning and getting excited about a shared vision and how we're going to work together."

That clarity, speed, and alignment locked the deal while others were still running spreadsheets.

Fast forward: WhatsApp now connects 2.7 billion monthly users and has become the communications infrastructure for half the planet. Street estimates put WhatsApp's contribution somewhere between $300-400 billion of Meta's market cap.

So, **was it overpriced?**

Only if you're still looking at the spreadsheet. Only if you think business is just math.

What do I see here?

Transformative deals don't go to the highest bidder.

They go to the clearest story. The fastest mover. The buyer who makes the founder feel like the match is inevitable.

And when competitive heat enters the room? That story better be airtight and delivered with conviction.

Sometimes the "craziest" price tag becomes the biggest bargain in hindsight. Just ask Instagram. Just ask YouTube. Just ask the companies who passed because the multiples "didn't make sense".

THE PSYCHOLOGY BEHIND STORYTELLING IN BUSINESS

We like to believe that, as buyers, we're rational – spreadsheet driven, immune to emotion, cool under pressure.

We're not.

At the end of the day, we're human. And humans don't buy based on logic alone. We buy based on stories that make us feel something – pride, fear, curiosity, desire.

Want proof?

The $128 Vase That Was Worth $1.49

In one of my all-time favourite studies, writers Rob Walker and Joshua Glenn conducted the **Significant Objects Project2.**

Here's what they did:

They bought 100 random trinkets off eBay. We're talking total junk – think plastic horses, used salt shakers, ceramic cats. The kind of stuff you'd see at a garage sale and still pass on.

Total spend? About $1.25 per item.

Then they did one simple thing:

They asked writers to pen **short stories** about each object.

Fictionalised histories that created allure. A backstory. A sense of meaning.

Then they listed the same junk items back on eBay – this time with the story included in the product description.

The results?

> A snow globe bought for 99 cents resold for $59
>
> A ceramic horse head went for $62 after being bought for $1.29
>
> A thrift-store vase, bought for $1.49, sold for $128

Across the board, the experiment yielded an **astonishing 6,395% return** on the original investment. Total spend: $128. Total resale value: **over $8,000.**

Same objects.

Same photos.

The only difference? **The story.**

Why This Works: Emotion Beats Logic (Almost Every Time)

Stories work because they tap into the part of the brain that spreadsheets don't reach.

They trigger **empathy, imagination,** and **identity.**

A compelling narrative helps a buyer imagine themselves as part of something larger:

- The **trailblazer** who makes the bold acquisition
- The **visionary** who spots value others missed
- The **leader** who drives transformation from the inside

Even in high-stakes M&A, decision-making is rarely cold. The math might back it up, but the **decision happens in the gut.**

A great story bridges the rational and the emotional.
It says:

"Yes, the numbers work – but here's why this deal matters."

It makes the buyer feel smart, strategic, and occasionally even a little legendary.

And that feeling? That's what gets deals **done.**

It's not a fluke. It's how the brain works.

Psychologists have shown that we **perceive things as better when they cost more.** In blind wine taste tests, people consistently rate the same wine higher when told it's expensive. The $10 bottle becomes a 94-point masterpiece – *if the story backs the price.*

And we're weird in the other direction, too.

Ever bought something just because it was on sale? Not because you needed it, but because the deal made you *feel* smart? That's all story, too. A narrative of value, scarcity, and "winning".

This is how buyers approach acquisitions. They want the deal to make them feel smart. Strategic. Ahead of the curve. Like they're buying something valuable *before* the rest of the market catches on.

Spreadsheets don't give you that feeling. **Stories do.**

That's why the most successful founder exits aren't driven by what your business has done. They're driven by the future your buyer *believes* your business will help them create.

THE THREE STORIES EVERY FOUNDER MUST MASTER

We humans are storytelling animals.

Long before spreadsheets and due diligence rooms, we

survived by sharing stories – around fires, in caves, later in boardrooms. Stories helped us remember what mattered and avoid what killed us.

And while we're naturally great at bad-news storytelling (it's how we evolved to stay alive), in business – especially when it's time to sell – you need to get equally great at *good-news storytelling*.

Why? Because the stakes are high – and for you, by now, they're likely to be exceptionally high. And buyers, they don't want numbers. They want meaning. They want to *feel* something.

You want them to experience hope. Clarity. Excitement. Safety.

If you can't give them that, they'll invent a story of their own. And it probably won't end in a premium multiple.

So before you hand over your pitch deck or start talking TAM and CAC, nail these three stories:

Origin Story: Why this business? Why you?

Growth Story: What value have you built and proven?

Future Story: What does their world look like with you inside it?

When you can deliver all three, you stop being just another company for sale, and start being a narrative they need to own.

Here's how to master these three distinct narratives so that buyers want in (and pay up).

1. Your origin story – why you built this business

Great origin stories create emotional connection. They explain not just what you built, but why you built it – the problem you saw, the insight you had, and the gap you filled.

When Tristan Walker sold Walker & Company (makers of Bevel) to Procter & Gamble, his origin story – creating grooming products specifically for people of colour after his own frustrating experiences – wasn't just backstory. It was a critical element that helped P&G recognise the massive unaddressed market they had been missing.

What you know is that your business didn't drop from the sky. You started it for a reason.

Maybe it was passion.

Maybe it was purpose.

Maybe it was pure frustration at how badly the problem was being handled.

(Or all three. That's usually the magic combo.)

Whatever your motivation, this is where your story starts. And you want your buyers to **feel it.**

Because no one gets excited about "we saw a gap in the market and launched a product." They get excited about *why* that gap mattered to you – and *how* you were uniquely qualified to fill it.

Your origin story should highlight:

- The specific problem you saw in the world
- Why existing solutions weren't cutting it
- The insight or unfair advantage you had
- The early spark of validation that proved you were onto something

We're not just talking backstory here. This is your **foundation.** It's the reason everything that came after makes sense.

When done well, your origin story doesn't just explain your business – it makes it feel inevitable.

The buyer hears it and thinks,

"Of course this worked.

Of course it's valuable.

I want in."

2. Your growth story – how you created value (and why it keeps working)

This isn't a "look how big we are" section. Size does matter, but *trajectory* is what gets buyers excited.

Almost anyone can build a rocket. But buyers want to see that you've cleared the launchpad – and that your engines are still firing. They're not buying where you are; they're buying where you're headed. Is it the moon (like Sir Peter Beck of Rocket Lab), or a fiery inferno (like Chris Kemp of Astra)?

Your growth story should make one thing obvious: luck has nothing to do with this – you've built a *system*. You've figured out how to attract the right customers, keep them coming back, and scale without the wheels falling off.

Here's what to show:

- Clear market validation (people genuinely want what you've built)
- Momentum that's building (no one-hit wonder vibes)
- Repeatable, scalable customer acquisition (bonus points if it works without you)
- Expanding value per customer (you're not just squeezing blood from a stone)
- Key inflection points that show this thing *really* works

Don't bore them with spreadsheets and graphs. Tell the story of how your revenue got smarter over time.

When Mihail and Georgi lined up SMS Bump for sale, they didn't just show a revenue number – they told a story. They showed how their CAC dropped while retention climbed. It was proof that their engine wasn't just running; it was compounding. That's the good stuff. That's what makes a buyer lean in and think, this thing will run even faster once we plug it into our machine.

Remember: you're not giving them a history lesson or reading out last quarter's news. You're showing them a crystal ball – and walking them through the future they want to buy into.

3. Your future story – what happens after acquisition

This is where most founders blow it.

They get so fixated on what they've built – how clever the product is, how impressive the growth looks – that they forget what buyers are buying.

Buyers aren't buying your past. They're buying their own future – with your business plugged into it.

So your job is to show them that future. With clarity, confidence, and a little bit of magic.

Your future story should paint a picture of:

- How your product fits into their strategic roadmap
- What you unlock for them that they couldn't get without you
- New revenue streams, new markets, or serious defensibility
- How you help them move faster, de-risk a bet, or leapfrog a competitor

You don't need a novel. You need a vision that makes the buyer sit back and say,

> *"If we don't buy this, our competitor will*
> *– and they'll eat our lunch."*

. . . .

Have you heard of Figma?

When Adobe dropped $20 billion to acquire them, Figma wasn't even a direct revenue threat. They were doing ~$400M ARR. Solid, but nothing Adobe couldn't squash in theory – they'd done it before.

As always, however, Adobe took the long view and it was grim. Figma owned the hearts and minds of the next generation of designers. They'd nailed multiplayer collaboration. They were browser-native, fast, loved, and growing like hell. And perhaps most importantly: Adobe couldn't build a credible competitor fast enough.

So Adobe paid ~50x revenue – one of the highest software multiples ever – for a story.

A story where they remained the undisputed design platform for the next 20 years. A story where they didn't get left behind by the cloud-native wave. A story where buying Figma wasn't just a product move – it was a survival strategy.

That's how you tell a future story.

You don't say, "We've done X so far." You say, "Here's what happens to **you** when this becomes part of **your** machine."

You're not just an acquisition. You're an **accelerant.** A crown jewel. The missing engine block in their next rocket ship.

So don't just ask, "How do I show them what I've built?"

Ask:

> *"How do I show them the future*
> *they can only get by acquiring us?"*

That's how you get them to pay up.

TAILORING YOUR STORY TO BUYER TYPES

> *"Don't tell me what you've built*
> *– show me what I'll own."*

A good narrative isn't just a founder monologue or a puffed-up pitch deck.

It's a buyer-specific story.

It answers their unasked questions, speaks their language, and makes them feel like saying **yes** would be the smartest move they've made all year.

Your job isn't to create a fantasy. It's to build a bridge between where the buyer is today and where they want to go, and then make it obvious that your company is the fastest, cleanest, and most elegant way to cross that bridge.

Using the **Buyer Motivation Matrix**™ from Chapter 5, here's how to tailor your three stories:

Strategic Buyers (Strategic Fit + Assets)

They want: Synergy, market share, distribution, competitive advantages

Your story emphasis:

- Origin: Focus on the strategic problem you solved that they still face

- Growth: Show market validation in their target segments
- Future: Paint the picture of combined market dominance

Financial Buyers (Financial Return + Assets)

They want: Stable cashflow, clean operations, predictable ROI

Your story emphasis:

- Origin: Highlight your focus on a sustainable business model
- Growth: Emphasise metrics, repeatability, and operational excellence
- Future: Show a clear path to continued cash generation

Acquihire Buyers (Strategic Fit + People)

They want: Your team to accelerate their existing initiatives

Your story emphasis:

- Origin: Focus on team formation and unique capabilities
- Growth: Show what your team has accomplished together
- Future: Demonstrate how your team plugs into their existing roadmap

Succession Buyers (Financial Return + People)

They want: Established operations and leadership continuity

Your story emphasis:

- Origin: Emphasise the systems and processes you've built

- Growth: Show that the business operates independently of the founder
- Future: Highlight continued stability and growth under new ownership

The best strategic buyers aren't obsessed with EBITDA. They're obsessed with answers to questions like:

"Does this help us **leapfrog a competitor?**"

"Can we bolt this on and instantly **unlock a new market?**"

"Does this get our CEO **out of hot water** with the board?"

Match your message to their motivations. If you try to tell the same story to every buyer, don't be surprised when none of them connect.

WEAPONISING YOUR NARRATIVE

Here's a point that may surprise you: **the buyer across the table isn't the one buying your business.** Not really.

They're your champion. Your interpreter. Your internal hype person. The one who's going to walk back into their boardroom, look the CEO in the eye, and say:

"This deal is a no-brainer."

And if it's not clear? You probably don't get to be in that room.

You don't get to explain the nuance. You don't get to field the tough questions or smooth over the eyebrow raises. All you get is what your narrative does **without** you.

So your job isn't just to build a compelling story.

It's to make that story **weaponisable** – repeatable, risk-reducing, and clear enough that someone else can pitch it better than you ever could.

Hit buyer fears before they voice them

If you've read Chapter 5, you already know what's keeping buyers up at night:

- Hidden skeletons
- Messy integrations
- Founders who **are** the business
- Strategic "sort of" fits that collapse under scrutiny

Don't wait for them to ask. Get ahead of the fear. Calm the lizard brain before it panics and kills the deal.

Examples:

- **Hidden Liabilities:** "We've completed a full financial and legal audit – clean as a whistle. No lawsuits, no backdoor clauses, no secret co-founder with 10% on a napkin."
- **Integration Risk:** "Here's our 90-day integration plan – people, tech, brand. It's Apple-level plug-and-play."
- **Founder Dependency:** "I haven't run ops in 12 months. The leadership team's been flying the plane. I'm here for vision, deals, and handover – then I'm off to Tulum."
- **Strategic Misalignment:** "Your earnings calls mention enterprise expansion. We already have warm doors into 14 of the top 100 – without you lifting a finger."

Pre-emptive clarity beats defensive explanations *every time*.

Make it re-sellable inside the buyer's organisation

Deals don't die in boardrooms because of a lack of logic. They die because your champion couldn't explain you in one sentence. Or worse – they **explained the wrong thing**.

So make it easy for them.

Make it easy for them to sell you.

Make it **simple. Sharable. Sharp:**

- A crisp one-pager they can share with stakeholders
- An internal deck with your integration roadmap, ROI model, and strategic fit bullets
- A 60-second "boardroom elevator pitch" they can say out loud and believe

Even the most excited champion still has to deal with a CFO who's allergic to risk, a CTO who hates surprise tech, and a board chair who's wondering why you're worth more than last year's budget.

I've seen founders create one-page "acquisition justification" documents specifically designed to help their buyer make the internal case for acquiring them. These founders understand that the sale happens within the buyer's organisation, not just in negotiations with you.

Make it easy for them to sell you.

YOUR STORYTELLING TOOLKIT

To make your story truly compelling and shareable, use these frameworks:

The Irresistible Narrative Template

1. **Problem**: What critical strategic challenge is the buyer facing?

2. **Solution**: How does your company uniquely solve this challenge?

3. **Proof**: What evidence demonstrates that your solution works?

4. **Future**: What becomes possible for the buyer after acquisition?

The Elevator Closer

Create a 60-second pitch that covers:

- The strategic problem you solve for this specific buyer
- Your unique approach and why it works
- The tangible value creation post-acquisition
- Why timing is critical (creating urgency)

The Acquisition Justification One-Pager

Create a document specifically designed to help your champion sell the acquisition internally, including:

- Strategic rationale (aligned with the buyer's public priorities)
- Integration roadmap and timeline
- Key risks and mitigation strategies
- Financial justification and ROI model

✔ FINAL CHECKPOINT FOR PART II IS YOUR NARRATIVE MAGNETIC OR MECHANICAL?

- Do you have a killer origin story that connects emotionally?
- Does your growth story show momentum – not just size?
- Have you built a future story that makes them the hero?
- Are you crafting the right story for the right type of buyer?
- Can your champion easily re-sell your narrative internally?

If you can't say yes to all five, you've now got the roadmap.

PART II CONCLUSION: STORIES CREATE VALUE

The highest-value acquisitions are driven by compelling stories that capture imagination and align with strategic visions. Whether it's Facebook buying WhatsApp or Adobe acquiring Figma, these deals prove that storytelling isn't just an art – it's a critical business skill that can redefine valuation dynamics in mergers and acquisitions.

Great businesses get acquired.

Irresistible businesses get pursued.

And pursued businesses? They don't just exit.

They exit on their terms.

That's the magic of the story.

Now that you know what story to tell, let's talk about how to execute it competitively...

The Power Dimension

CONTROLLING THE EXIT DYNAMIC

If you don't set the rules, someone else will.

CHAPTER 7

Create Competitive Tension

*"In business, you don't get what you deserve,
you get what you negotiate."*

– Chester L. Karrass

Have you ever bought or sold a house? If so, you've likely experienced the classic tactic: the real estate agent hints that "other buyers are interested," or urges you to hurry because "another offer has just come in." Even the most sceptical buyers feel that pressure. When multiple buyers enter the picture; whether real or imagined, everyone soon sharpens their bids. And you just know the end result; the seller almost always nets a higher price.

This isn't coincidence. Data shows homes with multiple offers sell for 10% to 20% more on average than similar properties with just one bid. The power behind this premium is competitive tension: the urgency, scarcity, and fear of missing out that drive buyers to act decisively and pay more. Whether you're selling a house or a business, the lesson is the same – engineer competition, create options, and build tension to dramatically improve your negotiating position and ultimate outcome.

Why do smart founders – people who've built valuable companies from nothing – suddenly become terrible negotiators when it's time to sell?

When Alex first received interest in his marketing technology company, the approach seemed perfect. A strategic buyer, solid cultural fit, initial offer of $18 million – reasonable for a business doing $3.2 million in revenue. The buyer was enthusiastic, the terms seemed fair, and Alex felt good about the potential partnership.

His advisor had different advice: "Never negotiate with just one buyer."

Alex was sceptical. Why complicate a good situation? The offer was already above market multiples. The buyer was someone he could see running his business well. Why risk damaging the relationship by bringing in competitors?

But Alex listened. And over the next four months, he engineered one of the most successful competitive processes I've witnessed. He mapped six strategic acquirers who would benefit from owning his technology. He'd built relationships with key executives at each company over the previous 18 months. He created pilot partnerships with two potential buyers to prove integration value. When formal interest emerged, he ran a structured process with clear timelines and maintained total transparency about the competitive nature throughout.

The financials didn't change. His revenue was still $3.2 million. His growth rate was the same. His team was identical.

But his valuation jumped to $31 million – a 72 % increase
purely through competitive tension.
That $13 million difference wasn't luck. It was strategy.

THE SINGLE-BUYER TRAP

The single most expensive mistake founders make in exits is negotiating with just one buyer – what I call "the single-buyer trap".

The trap is seductive because it seems logical. You're approached by a buyer who seems genuinely interested.

They're a good strategic fit. Their initial offer is within reasonable market range. Through early dialogue you develop good rapport and start to view them favourably as the future operator of your business. Why wouldn't you just work with them alone?

If it's not obvious: a single buyer has absolutely no incentive to offer their best price or terms.

None.

Without alternatives, you face an inherently unbalanced negotiation. The buyer controls timeline, applies pressure, and can gradually erode terms knowing you're already mentally committed.

By contrast, when multiple buyers are engaged simultaneously, each buyer knows they must present their most compelling offer, *you* control the timeline and urgency, and terms improve rather than erode as the process continues.

The impact of competitive tension on exits is dramatic and consistent. The pattern is clear: competitive tension doesn't just improve headline valuation. It improves every aspect of the exit, from structure to terms to timing to certainty. And

The key is approaching potential acquirers in a coordinated manner.

here's the critical insight: **you don't need dozens of potential buyers to create this dynamic.** Often, just two or three credible alternatives create sufficient tension to transform your outcome.

One of the clearest demonstrations of competitive tension comes from the world of startup funding. When a founder starts pitching for investment, responses are often lukewarm. Investors circle but rarely commit, each waiting for someone else to lead the way. All it takes to change the mood is a signal – typically a respected Angel or VC deciding to take a serious position in the round. Suddenly, the landscape shifts. Offers appear, timelines compress, and terms improve as other investors scramble to avoid missing out.

Like kids in the sandpit fighting over toys, there's a simple truth at play: <u>people want what others want</u>. A "whale" investor creates a ripple that draws in the rest of the market, often at better terms than you'd ever negotiate alone. The mere perception of competition triggers urgency and it's this engineered tension that consistently produces better deals.

This isn't unique to funding rounds. Whether you're seeking investment, hiring, or negotiating an exit, the lesson is the same: never negotiate with just one party. Create options, drive urgency, and let competitive tension work for you.

ENGINEERING YOUR BUYER ECOSYSTEM

Competitive tension doesn't happen by accident. It's deliberately engineered through a structured process that maximises your leverage.

Often, founders mistakenly fixate on a single type of buyer, usually the most obvious competitor. This narrow thinking severely limits competitive tension and your ultimate valuation.

Instead, expand your perspective using the **Buyer Motivation Matrix**™ from Chapter 5:

- **Strategic buyers** want synergy and competitive advantages
- **Financial buyers** want stable cashflow and predictable returns
- **Acquihire buyers** want your team to accelerate their existing initiatives
- **Succession buyers** want established operations with leadership continuity

Each category has different motivations, different pressure points, and different willingness to pay premiums.

The key is approaching potential acquirers in a coordinated manner.

Customise your positioning for each buyer type, emphasising what they value most. Maintain consistent timelines so all buyers move through the process together. Protect sensitive information through staged disclosure and appropriate confidentiality agreements. And manage communication flow to maintain your leverage throughout.

* * * * * * * * * * * * * * * * * *

Elena prepared to sell her enterprise software company by identifying buyer categories across multiple quadrants: strategic competitors who valued her customer base, technology platforms interested in her proprietary algorithms, and financial buyers attracted to her stable, recurring revenue. She wasn't playing games; she understood that different buyers would value different aspects of her business.

The most important element is creating **genuine urgency without manipulation.** Set clear process timelines and deadlines upfront. Communicate these consistently to all parties. Enforce deadlines without arbitrary extensions. Be transparent about the competitive nature of the process. Authentic urgency comes from a structured process, not from bluffing or artificial scarcity.

THE PSYCHOLOGY OF LEVERAGE

Your leverage position is largely established in the first interactions with potential buyers. Present from a position of strength and optionality. Demonstrate that you don't need to sell, even if you really want to. Establish clear parameters for engagement and set the framework for how information will be shared.

Leverage psychological principles

Successful negotiators understand and ethically leverage key psychological principles:

Loss Aversion (FOMO)

Buyers fear missing out on valuable opportunities more than they desire good deals. Frame your company as a scarce strategic asset and highlight unique capabilities that competitors can't replicate.

. . . .

Deidre positioned her manufacturing technology as "the only patented solution addressing this critical industry challenge" – emphasising uniqueness rather than just value. Each potential buyer recognised they might not just miss an opportunity, but potentially see it go to a competitor.

Emotional Investment

As buyers invest time and resources in evaluating your company, they become emotionally committed to completing the acquisition. Deepen this investment by engaging with their team at multiple levels and developing relationships with key decision-makers.

. . . .

Michael deliberately engaged with his acquirer's operational team, technology team, and executive leadership separately – creating multiple internal champions for the acquisition. By the time final negotiations occurred, the buyer had significant emotional investment across their organisation.

Michael faced a classic re-trade attempt when his primary buyer suddenly identified "customer concentration issues" two weeks before closing and proposed a 15% reduction in purchase price. Because Michael had maintained relationships with two other interested parties, he could credibly respond that he wasn't willing to renegotiate core terms. The buyer quickly dropped the request.

Steve had a different experience. With only one buyer, after 12 months of due diligence, at the signing ceremony they struck $1 million off the deal. Steve was beaten down and beaten; with no alternative available, he took the revised offer.

BUILDING LONG-TERM RELATIONSHIPS

The most successful competitive processes don't just focus on the exit at hand. They prioritise building relationships that create **ongoing optionality.**

Start building relationships early

Strategic relationships take time to develop. Begin cultivating connections with potential acquirers 18-24 months before you anticipate an exit:

- **Attend** industry conferences where potential buyers are present
- **Engage** in strategic partnerships that demonstrate integration value
- **Build** relationships with business development teams at target companies
- **Maintain** regular communication about industry trends and opportunities

Use partnership as a pathway

Strategic partnerships allow potential acquirers to experience your value first-hand while creating natural competitive dynamics:

- Pilot integrations that prove technical compatibility
- Joint go-to-market initiatives that demonstrate commercial synergy
- Co-development projects that show cultural alignment
- Revenue-sharing arrangements that validate economic benefits
- Alex's successful exit was built on 18 months of relationship building. Two of his eventual acquirers had started as integration partners, giving them first-hand experience of the value his technology could create within their platforms.

Position for strategic scarcity

Make your company feel like a unique strategic asset rather than one of many options:

- **Develop** proprietary technology or processes that are difficult to replicate
- **Build** exclusive relationships with key customers or partners
- **Create** network effects that become more valuable over time
- **Establish** thought leadership in your specific market niche

Your competitive tension checklist

Before engaging with potential buyers, ensure you have:

*Great exits aren't found,
they're created – through
deliberate strategy, skillful
negotiation, and the power of
genuine competitive tension.*

PROCESS FOUNDATION

- ☐ Identified 4-6 potential acquirers across multiple buyer categories
- ☐ Built relationships with key decision-makers over 12+ months
- ☐ Prepared buyer-specific positioning for each potential acquirer
- ☐ Established clear process timelines and deadlines

LEVERAGE OPTIMISATION

- ☐ Documented your negotiation boundaries and walk-away points
- ☐ Created authentic urgency without manipulation or bluffing
- ☐ Prepared responses to common buyer tactics and pressure points
- ☐ Maintained alternatives throughout the entire process

EXECUTION READINESS

- ☐ Customised your story for each buyer type using Chapter 6 frameworks
- ☐ Prepared one-page acquisition justifications for internal selling
- ☐ Established clear communication protocols and information flow
- ☐ Engaged appropriate advisors to manage complex negotiations

THE COMPETITIVE ADVANTAGE

Great exits aren't found, they're **created** – through deliberate strategy, skilful negotiation, and the power of genuine competitive tension. Remember: a buyer who knows they're your only option has no incentive to offer their best terms. A buyer who knows they're competing is motivated to put their best foot forward.

The difference between these scenarios often represents millions in exit value and significantly better terms. That difference isn't luck or timing – it's negotiation strategy. When you combine the storytelling frameworks from Chapter 6 with the competitive dynamics we've covered here, you create a foundation for extraordinary outcomes.

The key insight Alex discovered is that competitive tension isn't about manipulation or playing games. It's about creating a process where buyers *naturally compete* to offer their best terms, because they understand the value of what you've built and recognise they're not the only ones who see it.

Now that you know how to tell your story and create tension, the next critical question is understanding **what you want** from your exit...

✔ CHECKPOINT: ARE YOU READY TO PLAY?

- Have you identified multiple qualified buyers to create genuine competitive tension?
- Do you understand how to leverage buyer motivations and fears ethically?
- Are you confident negotiating earnouts, warranties, and non-competes?
- Do you have strategies to keep tension alive until the deal closes?
- Are your negotiation boundaries crystal clear?

CHAPTER 8

The Four Faces of Freedom

"Know yourself and you will win all battles."

– Sun Tzu

"The privilege of a lifetime is to become who you truly are."

– Carl Jung

What future life are you buying with an exit – and what would you regret leaving undone?

IN 2014...

... I was "happily" running my very successful IT services company. Or at least, that happy narrative was one that I had convinced myself of...

The reality was somewhat different.

For the previous two years, I'd taken the business on a full reinvention journey. We brought in a parade of consultants, completely refactored our offering, rebuilt capability across the team, and made a raft of new hires.

I invested over $1 million into the transformation. We even gave it a name: Project Moonshot – which, in hindsight, should've been a red flag about the odds of success.

By 2015, I was unwinding the entire thing. Making a tranche of people redundant. Ripping apart what we'd built. And yes – kicking over every rubbish bin in reach.

It all left me licking my wounds from the sizable financial (and emotional) loss.

I became miserable in my demeanour – and, if I'm honest, a miserable person to work with.

Thankfully, my minority business partner at the time had the character and courage to pull me aside and ask, "Are you okay?"

I wasn't.

That simple question kicked off a deep period of self-reflection. And eventually, I saw the truth: it wasn't the business that needed a dramatic change. It was me.

With that clarity, I made the decision to step away – not with a dramatic exit, but through a succession plan that preserved what we'd built and allowed the business to thrive without me at the helm. I wanted my team to be able to take this forward and share in the equity of its continued success.

It wasn't about chasing a headline valuation. It was about legacy. Continuity. Gracefully closing one chapter so the next one could begin – for the business, and for me.

As at writing this text, the business is 10 years older, carries the same name, is 500 % bigger, truly national, and I retain a great dividend-producing shareholding. I couldn't be happier.

WHY ONE-SIZE-FITS-ALL EXITS FAIL

The standard exit advice – maximise valuation, get all-cash, create competitive tension – isn't wrong. It's just *incomplete*. It assumes all founders want the same things, have identical risk appetites, and measure success the same way.

They don't.

I've worked with founders who happily accepted lower valuations for faster exits, others who walked away from premium offers to protect their team, and one who took 100% vendor finance and created an additional $200 million in wealth on his next venture.

These weren't mistakes. They were strategic choices made by people who knew what they needed beyond the money.

Most founders head into exit conversations with a broken compass.

They think they're being strategic – but really, they're just chasing the biggest number someone's willing to say out loud.

They focus on a single dimension – usually valuation – without realising that one priority pulls every other lever in the deal: timing, buyer type, structure, post-deal involvement, even how you feel about it once it's done.

In your defence, it's not surprising. Money is the most obvious, tangible, and fungible part of the deal. It's also the part that hits the headlines – and earns you high fives at the bowls club. The high likelihood though is that it's magpie bait. Flashy up front. Hollow underneath.

My hypothesis: we're using **the wrong mental model.** And let's be real: most people don't know what a mental model is. It sounds like something your McKinsey mate brings up over Negronis.

But it's simple: a mental model is just a way of seeing the world. **A lens.** A shortcut for making sense of complexity.

Charlie Munger called a "latticework of mental models" the highest form of intelligence. Why? Because when you only have one lens, aka *Maslow's Hammer*, everything starts to look like a nail.

If your only model for exits is "maximise valuation", then you'll:

- Wait too long
- Chase the wrong buyers
- Over-optimise your spreadsheet
- Under-prepare your story
- Maybe even win the deal... but regret the life that follows

It's why so many founders feel weird **after** a "successful" exit. They got the money. But they lost the plot.

They weren't playing the wrong game.

They were playing **someone else's.**

That's why I created the **Exit Archetypes.**

Not as a quiz. Not as a cute framework. But as a **practical tool** to help you define your own version of success – and make sure every move you make aligns with it.

Because exits don't just test your business.

They test your self-awareness.

INTRODUCING: THE FOUR EXIT ARCHETYPES

After working with hundreds of founders through exits, I've identified **four distinct founder archetypes,** each with different priorities, strengths, blind spots, and optimal exit strategies. **I'd like to share them with you now.**

The Maximiser

CORE PRIORITY: MAXIMUM FINANCIAL RETURN

Maximisers are defined by their relentless focus on achieving the highest possible exit valuation. They're willing to run extended processes, negotiate aggressively, and wait for the perfect strategic alignment to maximise their return.

Evan Goldberg's $9.3 billion exit to Oracle is a masterclass in the Maximiser playbook.

It didn't happen overnight. It took decades of positioning, patience, and playing the long game.

Evan founded NetSuite (originally NetLedger) in 1998 after a five-minute phone call with Larry Ellison – who became an early investor and later, the company's biggest shareholder. That connection, and the slow, deliberate expansion into ERP, e-comm, and vertical-specific tools, built NetSuite into a category leader.

They IPO'd. They proved the model. Then they waited.

In 2016, Oracle paid $109/share – 3–4 x higher than what financial buyers were offering. The deal came with none of the usual drama. Goldberg and Ellison both recused themselves to avoid conflict. The outcome? Clean. Strategic. High multiple. High alignment.

Today, NetSuite still runs as a thriving unit inside Oracle. In fact, Goldberg himself runs it – so the culture remains intact. Plus, the growth continues to compound.

It's a reminder: if you want a premium, you are likely to need more than numbers – you need leverage, relationships, and time.

MAXIMISER TRAITS:

- Highly analytical and detail-oriented
- Comfortable with complex deal structures
- Willing to walk away from good offers in pursuit of great ones
- Patient and strategic in developing buyer relationships
- Views the exit as the culmination of years of work and sacrifice

If it's not obvious: this deal type will take years.

OPTIMAL EXIT PATH FOR MAXIMISERS:

- Strategic acquisition with competitive tension
- Longer, more structured sale process
- Multiple potential acquirers
- Deal structures that maximise headline value, even with contingencies

The Closer

CORE PRIORITY: SPEED AND SIMPLICITY

Closers want a clean, fast, and uncomplicated exit. They prioritise speed and certainty over squeezing out the last dollar of valuation. For Closers, the perfect exit is one that closes quickly with minimal drama and clear finality.

Ryan Smith's sale of Qualtrics to SAP for $8 billion in 2018 exemplifies the Closer archetype, prioritising speed, simplicity, and certainty over potentially higher, but uncertain, returns. Founded in 2002 in Provo, Utah, Qualtrics was a family

venture operating from the Smith family basement.
Bootstrapping for a decade created a frugal mindset and keen
eye for deals.

In 2018, as Qualtrics prepared for an IPO, SAP presented an
all-cash acquisition offer of $8 billion. Smith accepted four days
before listing, favouring decisiveness, guaranteed outcome,
and a clean break.

CLOSER TRAITS:

- Decisive and action-oriented
- Values simplicity and clarity
- Often ready to move on to next chapter
- Pragmatic about valuation
- Prefers clean breaks over lingering commitments

OPTIMAL EXIT PATH FOR CLOSERS:

- All-cash or heavily front-loaded deals
- Minimal earnouts or contingencies
- Financial buyers who can move quickly
- Simplified due-diligence process
- Clear, clean transition plans

The Legacy Builder

CORE PRIORITY: IMPACT AND CONTINUITY

Legacy Builders care more about what happens to their company, team, and customers after the exit than about maximising their personal return. They view their business as their legacy and prioritise finding the right home over finding the highest bidder.

In 2022, Yvon Chouinard transferred Patagonia to a trust fighting climate change – he gifted his company to the planet.

Yvon never wanted to be a businessman. He was a climber and craftsman who proved business could work differently. Patagonia pioneered environmental responsibility and a work culture celebrating adventure.

His boldest move was structuring Patagonia so every dollar not reinvested goes directly to protecting the Earth.

"Earth is now our only shareholder."

LEGACY BUILDER TRAITS:

- Deeply attached to company mission and values
- Highly concerned with team welfare post-acquisition
- Often founder-CEOs of bootstrapped companies
- Views business as an extension of personal values
- Measures success by impact, not just financial return

OPTIMAL EXIT PATH FOR LEGACY BUILDERS:

- Strategic acquirer with aligned values and mission
- Succession or management buyouts
- Deals with explicit protections for team and culture
- Structured earnouts tied to non-financial metrics

The Equity Earner

CORE PRIORITY: ONGOING PARTICIPATION WITH REDUCED RISK

Equity Earners want to "take some chips off the table" while continuing the game. They seek partial liquidity that reduces personal financial risk while maintaining meaningful upside and involvement in the business's future growth.

Kevin Plank founded Under Armour in 1996. After stepping down as CEO in 2019, he remained Executive Chairman, keeping significant equity and influence.

In 2024 he returned to the CEO seat, demonstrating classic Equity Earner behaviour: preserve influence, protect upside, and keep the option to step back in.

EQUITY EARNER TRAITS:

- Enjoys building and operating businesses
- Seeks financial security without full exit
- Often younger founders with more runway ahead
- Values optionality and flexibility
- Comfortable with longer-term alignment

OPTIMAL EXIT PATH FOR EQUITY EARNERS:

- Search-fund path to equity
- Private-equity partnerships with founder rollover
- Strategic minority investments
- Structured earnouts with operational autonomy
- Growth-equity recapitalisations
- Holding-company structures enabling multiple ventures

ALIGNING YOUR ARCHETYPE WITH YOUR EXIT STRATEGY

Knowing your Exit Archetype isn't just an interesting snippet of self-knowledge. It's a **strategic advantage** that shapes every aspect of your exit.

For Maximisers:

Focus on **building relationships** with strategic buyers who can pay premium multiples. Invest in competitive positioning that creates FOMO among potential acquirers. Be willing to run longer processes with multiple parties to maximise tension.

For Closers:

Prepare extensively before going to market so when offers come, you can move quickly. Consider financial buyers who value certainty and speed. Create clean, straightforward deal structures that minimise post-close entanglements.

For Legacy Builders:

Identify potential acquirers with **truly aligned values.** Document critical cultural elements that must be preserved. Consider alternative structures like employee ownership or mission-aligned investors.

For Equity Earners:

Explore private-equity partnerships that allow significant founder rollover. Structure deals with clear operational autonomy and defined decision rights. Create explicit mechanisms for **eventual full liquidity** down the road.

Common archetype mistakes (and how to avoid them)

Maximiser Mistakes	• Overplaying their hand • Analysis paralysis • Valuing price over terms
Closer Mistakes	• Signalling desperation • Skipping preparation • Accepting unnecessary contingencies
Legacy Builder Mistakes	• Trusting verbal commitments • Limiting buyer pool • Post-sale meddling
Equity Earner Mistakes	• Structural complexity • Role confusion • Partner misalignment

YOUR EXIT ARCHETYPE TOOLKIT

Quick diagnostic: which archetype are you?

Ask yourself these four questions:

1. If you had to choose one, which would you prefer?

☐ **A:** The highest possible valuation, even if it takes longer and involves more complexity

☐ **B:** A fast, clean exit, even if the valuation is somewhat lower

☐ **C:** Ensuring your team, culture, and mission continue, even at a discount

☐ **D:** Taking some chips off the table while staying involved with significant upside

2. What would cause you the most regret in an exit?

☐ **A:** Leaving money on the table

☐ **B:** A long, drawn-out process with an uncertain outcome

☐ **C:** Seeing your company's culture or mission destroyed post-acquisition

☐ **D:** Giving up control and missing out on future growth

3. How do you feel about post-acquisition involvement?

☐ **A:** I want a clean break to pursue new opportunities

☐ **B:** I'll help with a short, defined transition, then move on

☐ **C:** I care deeply about staying involved to protect the legacy

☐ **D:** I want to maintain meaningful operational involvement with upside

4. What matters most in your buyer?

☐ **A:** Ability to pay the highest possible price

☐ **B:** Capability to close quickly and cleanly

☐ **C:** Alignment with your values and commitment to your team

☐ **D:** Willingness to structure a deal with ongoing founder participation

Your answers will typically point to a primary archetype, though many founders are hybrids of two adjacent types.

✔ CHECKPOINT: WHAT'S YOUR TRUE ARCHETYPE?

Which archetype resonates most strongly with you – Maximiser, Closer, Legacy Builder, or Equity Earner?

- Is your current exit strategy aligned with your archetype's true priorities?
- Have you thought through potential misalignments and how to avoid common archetype mistakes?
- Are you clear about which types of buyers fit best with your archetype?
- If you have co-founders, do you have alignment on your exit archetypes, or are you pursuing conflicting paths?
- Understanding your Exit Archetype isn't about limiting your options. It's about ensuring that the exit you pursue delivers what truly matters to you – not just what conventional wisdom says you should want. Because the most successful exits aren't just measured by the number on the wire transfer. They're measured by how well they align with who you really are.

So before you build your data room, pause. Ask yourself: what kind of founder are you?

Because exits don't just test your business – **they reveal your truth.**

"Your decisions reveal your priorities."

– Stephen Covey

CHAPTER 9

The Flywheel and the Window

"Luck is what happens when preparation meets opportunity."

– Seneca

If that dream buyer called tomorrow, how quickly could you prove your company is worth what you think it is?

. . . .

In 2019, Nirmal "Nims" Purja announced a plan which made seasoned mountaineers spit their freeze-dried meals all over their tent in hilarity.

He was going to climb all 14 of the world's highest peaks – every mountain over 8,000 meters – in six months. For context, the previous record was nearly eight years. Most climbers spend their entire careers attempting maybe three or four of these peaks. Even then, roughly 10% of them don't make it home.

"If you believe, everything is possible", Nims said. The climbing establishment thought he'd been oxygen deprived for too long. They were wrong.

Six months and six days later, Nims had done the impossible. Not because he got lucky with perfect weather on all 14 peaks. Because he'd built a systematic approach that worked regardless of conditions.

While other climbers were waiting for perfect conditions on one mountain, Nims was creating momentum across the entire project. He treated all 14 peaks as an integrated system where each climb built momentum for the next. His preparation was methodical. His timing was strategic.

What really separated Nims from traditional climbers was this: he understood that systematic preparation is only half the equation. The other half is recognising when conditions align for your summit push.

I know two founders who learned this lesson. One the easy way, one the hard way.

· · · · · · · · · · · · · · · · · · · ·

When the construction boom peaked in 2019, the first founder moved fast. His books were clean, processes documented, buyer relationships warm. Within three months, he'd closed at a healthy multiple.

His competitor saw the same opportunity but wasn't prepared. "I need another quarter to get my financials sorted," he said. "The market's hot – it'll wait."

It didn't. Six years later, that founder is still trying to find buyers.

Same industry, similar companies, completely different outcomes. One understood that exceptional exits require both systematic preparation and strategic timing.

YOUR EXIT IS YOUR "14 PEAKS"

Building and selling a business is a lot like Nims' Project Possible. Founders habitually approach their exit like traditional climbers – they build their company, then hope that buyers, market conditions, and timing all align for one perfect exit moment.

The founders who achieve exceptional exits don't rely on hope. They use what I call the **Exit Flywheel** – a systematic approach that builds momentum across four integrated phases. But unlike traditional business frameworks, the flywheel is designed to work *with* market timing, not against it.

Just like Nims didn't wait for perfect weather, smart founders don't wait for perfect market conditions. They create their own momentum while staying alert for when the summit window opens.

THE EXIT FLYWHEEL MEETS YOUR EXIT WINDOW

The Exit Flywheel is your systematic preparation – four phases that build compounding momentum toward an exceptional exit:

Phase 1: Building Value: Like Nims' physical training, this is where you build the foundation that makes everything else possible.

Phase 2: Exit Readiness: Your gear check. Sorting financials, systems, and processes before the pressure hits.

Phase 3: Creating Buyer Tension: Positioning so buyers know they're competing for you, not evaluating you.

Phase 4: Execution: The summit push. Getting the deal done without losing leverage or your mind.

But here's what founders have a tendency to miss: the flywheel alone isn't enough. You also need to recognise your **Exit Window** – those brief moments when industry dynamics, market conditions, and personal factors align to create optimal exit conditions.

The magic happens when **systematic preparation meets strategic timing.** Your flywheel creates the capability. Reading the window correctly captures the value.

Too often do founders treat preparation and timing as separate considerations. Smart founders understand they're part of the same system.

The Four Phases of the Exit Flywheel

Unlike a linear checklist, the Flywheel is dynamic. Each phase amplifies the next, creating compounding momentum that makes buyers chase you instead of the other way around.

PHASE 1: BUILDING VALUE

This is your **base camp training.** You're building a business that doesn't just run – it climbs under its own steam.

We're talking revenue growth with a story behind it. Clear product-market fit that proves you've solved a real problem in a scalable way. Tangible, transferable intellectual assets – systems, processes, and knowledge that don't live exclusively in your head. A team that can execute without you. Some form of competitive moat, even a small one.

The better your foundation here, the smoother everything that follows.

PHASE 2: EXIT READINESS

Your **gear check.** Financial hygiene and reliable reporting. Legal housekeeping. Documented systems that prove your business runs on more than founder intuition. Customer concentration addressed. Clean governance trail.

Founders who excel at Phase 2 make their value immediately apparent to buyers, reduce perceived risk, accelerate due diligence, and ultimately increase the size of the check they cash at closing.

PHASE 3: CREATING BUYER TENSION

In this phase, you're **engineering leverage** by cultivating relationships with multiple potential acquirers. As we covered in Chapter 7, this is about positioning so that buyers know they're competing for you, not evaluating you. You stop chasing offers. The offers chase *you*.

PHASE 4: EXECUTION

The **summit push** – covered in detail in Chapters 11-13. This is where you're managing negotiations, due diligence, and the complex psychology of closing while preserving your leverage and sanity.

THE SUMMIT

Nims' incredible achievement and multiple world records were the result. The backstory is that systematic preparation beats hoping for perfect conditions every single time.

While other climbers were still arguing about whether his goal was even possible, Nims was already standing on his 14th summit, planting the Nepalese flag on Shishapangma. Not because he was lucky. Not because the weather was perfect. Because he'd built a system that worked regardless of conditions.

The Exit Flywheel works the same way. You'll recall that founders spend 40,000 hours building their business on average, but barely 100 hours planning their exit. Then they wonder why they don't get the outcome they deserve.

It's not about timing the perfect moment or finding the perfect buyer. It's about building momentum across four phases so that when your window opens – and it will open – you're not scrambling to get ready. **You're already there.**

Most founders treat their exit like an afterthought. They hope someone notices their value, hope the market timing works out, hope they don't screw up the negotiations.

Hope is not a strategy.

Nims proved that audacious goals become achievable when you approach them systematically. Your exit is no different. Build the flywheel, trust the process, and when you plant your flag at the summit, you'll know it wasn't luck.

It was **preparation meeting opportunity.**

TIMING ISN'T EVERYTHING (IT'S THE ONLY THING)

As both an investor and founder, I've learnt this the hard way: when it comes to selling your business, timing isn't just important – it's everything. You can get everything else right; stellar products, elite team, growing numbers, buyers who love you. But if you mistime the move?

Game over.

Sell too early and you leave millions on the table. Wait too long and you watch millions vanish before your eyes.

Founders have a habit of thinking of an exit as a finish line. A moment they'll "just know" has arrived.

But that's not how it works.

A great exit is not a moment. It's a mountain.

And timing is the weather.

THE HOURGLASS EFFECT (WHEN WINDOWS CLOSE FAST)

One of the most painful experiences I consistently witness is what I call the **Hourglass Effect:** when a founder's exit window closes much faster than anticipated, sometimes dramatically reducing valuation potential.

Think of your exit potential as sand in an hourglass. In some cases, the sand drains slowly and predictably. In others, the hourglass suddenly flips, and value drains rapidly.

Several factors can trigger this sudden closure:

Disruptive Market Entrants

When major players enter your space, windows can close with stunning speed. I watched a founder reject a $40 million offer, only to see his valuation drop to under $20 million twelve months later when an aggressive, well-funded global player eroded their market share.

Rapid Investor Sentiment Shifts

Investor appetite for specific sectors can change virtually overnight. During the 2022 tech correction, SaaS valuations in certain segments dropped from 15-20x revenue to 4-6x in a matter of months. Founders who had been building toward exits found their windows slammed shut.

Regulatory Changes

New regulations or enforcement priorities can transform an attractive sector into a challenging one almost overnight. Healthcare technology, financial services, and privacy-related businesses are particularly vulnerable to these sudden shifts.

Founder Burnout

Perhaps the most underappreciated factor in the Hourglass Effect is founder burnout. When founder energy depletes, business performance typically follows – often creating a downward spiral that accelerates as valuation potential erodes.

I worked with a founder who was experiencing increasing burnout but decided to "push through" for another year to improve his company's metrics. During that year, his disengagement led to leadership gaps, slowing growth, and increasing customer churn. By the time he decided to sell, his valuation had decreased by nearly 35%.

The lesson is clear: Windows don't just close – sometimes they slam shut. The cost of missing your Window often far exceeds the incremental value you might build by waiting.

✔ CHECKPOINT: EXIT STRATEGY OR AFTERTHOUGHT?

- Do you clearly understand where your business sits on the Exit Flywheel today?
- If your exit window suddenly opened tomorrow, would you be ready to move?
- Are you maintaining the energy and commitment needed to maximise value, or is founder fatigue becoming a factor?
- What specific market signals would cause you to accelerate your exit timeline?

Remember: The perfect exit isn't about achieving some hypothetical future state of business perfection. It's about hitting the sweet spot where your **Flywheel Momentum** aligns with your **optimal Exit Window.**

> *"The flywheel turns slowly at first,*
> *then gains unstoppable energy."*
>
> – Jim Collins

Now that you understand your archetype and can read market timing, the next question is strategic positioning: how do you present yourself to maximise your specific type of freedom?

CHAPTER 10

Stop Making Million-Dollar Mistakes: The Exit Quadrant™

"All models are wrong, but some are useful."

– George Box

"You can have anything you want, but not everything at once."

– Naval Ravikant

You built smart. Do you really want to exit stupid?

In Chapter 8, we identified which of the four archetypes you are: **Maximiser, Closer, Legacy Builder,** or **Equity Earner.** You know what drives you, what you value beyond money, and what kind of freedom you're chasing.

Now comes the harder question: How do you design an exit that *delivers it*?

Picture this scenario: You're sitting in your office on a Tuesday afternoon. Your business has been performing well – solid growth, healthy margins, a team that gets along.

An acquisition offer lands in your inbox.

You should be excited. This is what you've been building toward, right?

Instead, you're staring at the term sheet feeling completely lost.

Is this a good offer?

Should I wait for something better?

What if this is my only shot?

What if I take it and regret it for the rest of my life?

That paralysing mix of *opportunity* and *doubt* happens when you've spent years learning how to build a business but zero time learning how to **exit** one.

I've seen founders stuck in exits that last two painful years longer than necessary because they chased every last dollar. I've watched others sell their business in days, then spend years regretting how much money they left on the table. Some exit confidently, only to realise they traded certainty for chaos. Others cling to control, only to discover it cost them opportunities and freedom.

Why do smart, strategic people consistently make these mistakes?

Because they're flying blind. They think the only question is "How much can I sell for?" But that's just one piece of a much bigger puzzle.

An exit isn't one-dimensional. It's a delicate balancing act between four equally crucial factors:

- **Speed:** How quickly can you close the deal? How long do you need to stick around afterwards?
- **Valuation:** How high can you push the number?
- **Control:** How much involvement or influence do you retain after the exit?

- **Certainty:** How predictable, structured, and guaranteed are the terms?

Most founder regret comes from optimising for one dimension while ignoring the others. Like the founder who pushed for that extra million, only to watch his team culture get dismantled during the 14-month closing process. Or the founder who took the quick-and-easy private equity deal, only to realise she'd signed up for five years of diminishing control and mounting frustration.

But before we dive into the framework that prevents these mistakes, we need to talk about something deeper: the mental traps that sabotage even the smartest founders.

THE FOUR MENTAL TRAPS THAT WRECK EXITS

As you'll recall in Chapter 8, Charlie Munger called mental models "a latticework" for good decision-making. When you only have one lens – and that lens is money – everything starts looking like a dollar sign.

These are the biases that cost founders **millions, years,** or **their sanity:**

1. Sunk Cost Fallacy (Kills Speed)

> *"I've put too much into this to walk away now."*

You overvalue what you've already invested – money, time, identity – even when those costs can't be recovered. This keeps you hanging on too long, waiting for some mythical payoff that justifies the pain.

The damage: You miss your moment. Markets shift. Teams get tired. The asset starts declining while you're still chasing yesterday's dream.

Reality check: Ask yourself, "Would I start this exit process today, knowing what I know now?"

2. Availability Heuristic (Distorts Valuation)

"My mate got 15x ARR. Why shouldn't I?"

Your brain anchors on the most vivid story, not the most accurate data. When someone in your network sells for a crazy multiple, that becomes your benchmark – **even if their situation was completely different.**

The damage: You overreach on price, scare away real buyers, and get stuck chasing ghosts.

Reality check: Use actual market data, not LinkedIn headlines, to set expectations.

3. Status Quo Bias (Destroys Timing)

"It's not perfect timing. Maybe I'll wait."

You default to "not now" because it feels safer than change; even when change could unlock your next chapter. This delay often masquerades as strategy when it's really just fear.

The damage: You miss market windows. Buyers lose interest. Opportunities evaporate while you're still "getting ready".

Reality check: Ask, "Am I staying because it's right, or because I'm afraid of what comes next?"

4. Illusion of Control (Breeds False Certainty)

"I'll stay involved and make sure it all goes smoothly."

You assume that post-exit, you'll still call the shots. But once the money's wired, influence fades fast – especially if your role isn't crystal clear upfront.

The damage: You end up in messy post-acquisition limbo, frustrated and powerless to influence what you care about most.

Reality check: Be brutally honest about how much control matters to you, then contract for it or *let it go*.

These mental traps don't show up as conscious decisions. They show up as procrastination, perfectionism, or pushing too hard for the wrong deal.

Which brings us to the solution.

ENTER THE EXIT QUADRANT™

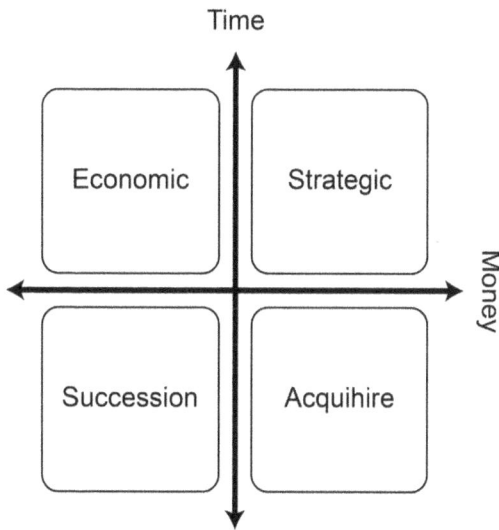

There's no such thing as a "perfect" exit. There's only the *right* exit – for you, your stakeholders, and your life after.

The problem? Founders don't realise what they're trading off until they're already neck-deep in due diligence, earnout clauses, and board calls they regret taking.

That's why I created the **Exit Quadrant**™ – a decision-making framework that helps you see the trade-offs clearly before you're sitting across from a buyer.

The Two Axes That Matter

The quadrant maps across two real-world dimensions:

VERTICAL AXIS: TIME TO EXIT

How long from "I want to sell" to "deal signed". The higher you go, the longer it takes.

HORIZONTAL AXIS: FINANCIAL OUTCOME

The valuation or total payout. The further right you go, the more money you make.

Simple enough. But here's where it gets interesting: these two factors are usually inversely related. Want maximum dollars? Plan to invest maximum time. Need speed? Expect to leave money on the table.

With those axes in place, four distinct exit types emerge – each with different trade-offs, different buyers, and different outcomes.

Economic Exit (Top Left: Slow + Mid-Money)

This is where founders tend to land by **default** – not by **design.**

A financial buyer runs a slow, forensic process. Due diligence is exhaustive. The multiple ends up average or below. They don't care about your story, your team, or your vision; just your EBITDA.

Common traits:

- High-friction due diligence
- Valuation based on trailing financials

- Little post-deal founder influence
- Buyers focused purely on numbers

Most regret lives here. It's the exit you get when you don't prepare, don't position, and don't create any buyer tension.

Strategic Exit (Top Right: Slow + Big Money)

This is the **aspirational exit.** Done right, it's the most lucrative – and often the most fulfilling.

Strategic acquirers pay premiums not just for your financials, but for your narrative, IP, customer base, or market position. They're buying what you unlock for their business.

Common traits:

- Top-quartile market multiples
- Clear synergies that drive value
- Competitive tension can push price higher
- Buyer genuinely values your strategic assets

The holy grail for **Maximisers** and the right path for founders willing to invest in positioning, patience, and story.

Succession Exit (Bottom Left: Fast + Mid-Money)

This is the **cleanest** and often the **kindest** exit path.

Management buyouts, partner sales, or family succession. Fast to close, low friction, strong cultural alignment. The valuation is fair but not inflated, and there's usually goodwill baked into the deal.

Common traits:

- Fastest time to close
- Strong cultural continuity

- Low due diligence overhead
- Business strategy stays intact

Perfect for **Legacy Builders** or **Closers** who aren't chasing top dollar and want to see the business thrive post-sale.

Acquihire Exit (Bottom Right: Fast + High Money)

This is the quadrant most founders wish they were in but **rarely reach by accident.**

Premium exits based on team, reputation, and market buzz rather than just financials. If the buyer wants your people or your brand, they'll move fast and pay well.

Common traits:

- Lightning-fast timeline
- Often driven by buyer FOMO
- Valuation may match Strategic Exit – without the long road
- Focus on talent and intangible assets

Smart target for **Closers** or **Equity Earners** who've built assets beyond the balance sheet.

ALIGNING YOUR ARCHETYPE WITH YOUR EXIT QUADRANT™

Every founder shows up to exit with a different appetite for risk, reward, and reinvention. That's why there's no one-size-fits-all path. Regrets surface when pursuing a deal that doesn't align with the founder's true nature.

Now that you know the four exit types, which one fits your archetype from Chapter 8?

The Maximiser → Strategic Exit

Maximisers play the long game for premium returns.

Strategic Exit rewards patience and positioning, but watch out for over-optimising and losing momentum while chasing the perfect deal.

The Closer → Acquihire or Succession Exit

Closers want speed and simplicity.

Acquihire works if you've built strong team/brand assets.

Succession is the fastest, friendliest path. Just don't leave significant value on the table by rushing without any competitive tension.

The Legacy Builder → Succession or Strategic Exit

Legacy Builders prioritise continuity over cash.

Succession offers values alignment and cultural continuity.

Strategic Exit works if you find a buyer who genuinely shares your mission. The trap? Trusting buyers who say the right things but won't deliver.

The Equity Earner → Acquihire or Strategic Exit

Equity Earners want liquidity with ongoing participation. Both paths can offer continued involvement and shared upside. The risk? Complex deals with unclear authority that leaves you stuck between full control and none.

The biggest mistakes happen when archetypes chase the wrong quadrant: Closers getting trapped in drawn-out strategic processes, or Legacy Builders ending up in purely transactional economic exits.

The Danger Zone: Economic Exit

You may have noticed that there's one quadrant we haven't mapped to any archetype yet. There's a reason for that.

Economic Exit doesn't align with anyone's true priorities.

It's the **slowest.**

It's the **driest.**

It's the **most rigid.**

It's the **least generous.**

Think about it:

- **Maximisers** want premium returns – Economic Exit delivers average multiples
- **Closers** want speed – Economic Exit takes the longest
- **Legacy Builders** want cultural alignment – Economic Exit treats business as commodity
- **Equity Earners** want ongoing participation – Economic Exit offers the least flexibility

Yet this is where **founders often end up.** Not because they chose it, but because they never made a conscious choice at all.

The real danger isn't the quadrant itself – it's ending up there **by default.**

When you don't intentionally target a quadrant that fits your archetype, you drift toward whoever happens to find you first. Usually a financial buyer running a slow, forensic process focused purely on historical numbers.

The antidote is simple: Know which quadrant you're targeting before anyone ever contacts you. Because once you're in someone else's process, you're playing their game, by their rules.

Choose your quadrant deliberately, or **someone else will choose it for you.**

EXIT QUADRANT™ CHECKPOINT

Before you take another meeting or sign another NDA, get **crystal clear** on these questions:

Which quadrant aligns with your true priorities?

Speed vs. money isn't the only trade-off. Factor in control, certainty, and what you want your life to look like after.

Do you understand what you're trading off?

Every quadrant has costs. Maximisers trade time for money. Closers trade money for speed. Legacy Builders trade maximum returns for continuity. Be honest about what you're willing to give up.

Is your current approach targeting the right quadrant?

If you're a Closer but chasing a Strategic Exit, you're setting yourself up for frustration. If you're a Legacy Builder drifting toward Economic Exit, you'll regret it.

Are you and your stakeholders aligned?

Co-founders, investors, and key team members might have different quadrant preferences. Get this sorted before you're negotiating with buyers.

"In the absence of a strategy,
we default to doing what comes easiest."

– Clayton Christensen

"Play long-term games
with long-term people."

– Naval Ravikant

The Exit Quadrant™ isn't about finding the "best" exit – it's about finding your best exit. The one that aligns with what you truly value, not just what conventional wisdom says you should want.

So before you spend a single hour in your data room, take the time to step back and reflect. Ask yourself: *What quadrant is this buyer leading me into? And is it where I want to end up?*

Because the most powerful position in any exit isn't the one with the biggest number – it's the one where you're making every trade-off consciously, with your eyes wide open.

✔ CHECKPOINT: FIND YOUR BEST EXIT

- Are you stuck on the idea of a "perfect" exit? Why?

- Which "mental trap" do you need to guard against the most? How will you do it?

- If you were forced to choose, would you rather get more money or instant freedom?

- Are you ready to accept that your best exit might mean walking away from greater financial freedom?

- How important is the future success of the team you've built to support the achievement of your vision?

- If you're already in conversation with a buyer, what tactics can you adopt to move them away from an economic exit?

CHAPTER 11

Going Solo vs. Going Pro: The True Cost of Amateur Hour

"You can't read the label from inside the jar."

– Anonymous

I f you needed to have complex surgery, would you chat to AI for an hour for a DIY solution? Or locate the best surgeon available?

RED ADAIR: THE MAN WHO CONQUERED HELL FOR A LIVING

Red Adair puts out fires. Not your backyard barbecue or even a burning building. Specifically, oil well fires. Imagine literal geysers of fire shooting hundreds of feet into the air, fuelled by pressurised oil and gas erupting from deep within the earth. Infernos that could burn for months, destroy millions in assets, and kill anyone who got too close.

When most people would run away, Red would walk straight toward the flames.

He stood 5'7" with his flaming red hair (yes, that's where the nickname came from), but he cast a shadow larger than life. From the 1950s until he retired in the 1990s, Adair and his team – always dressed in their signature red overalls – were the global 911 call for the world's most dangerous fires.

Kuwait, 1991, is one such example and a legendary part of oil industry history. Saddam Hussein's retreating army had set over 700 oil wells ablaze, creating an apocalyptic hellscape. Black smoke turned day into night. Lakes of oil burned across the desert. Temperatures near the wellheads reached 2,000 degrees. Red, in his mid-70s at that point, was among the first specialists called in.

Was he well-compensated? Absolutely. Red once said, "If you think it's expensive to hire a professional, wait until you hire an amateur." Companies paid millions for his services, and they considered it a bargain.

Red understood something most people miss: when everything's on the line, expertise isn't expensive – it's essential.

Yes, I've said this before. No, I'm not sorry: The average founder spends over 40,000 hours building their business before exit. Yet they'll dedicate less than 100 hours to planning how that exit unfolds.

Your exit is your oil fire moment. Everything you've built is at stake. The wrong move can cost you millions, destroy what you've created, or leave you trapped in a deal you'll regret for years.

Yet most founders try to handle it themselves.

THE MYTH OF SAVING MONEY BY GOING SOLO

The biggest disasters I've seen
came from founders who went solo.

– Neil Millar, Top M&A Lawyer

The decision to handle your own exit typically stems from three seductive beliefs:

"Advisors are too expensive." A $10 million exit might include $300,000 to $500,000 in total advisory fees. That feels like real money.

"I know my business better than anyone." You've built this company, negotiated countless deals, understand every detail. Surely selling is just another negotiation?

"How hard can it be?" Find a buyer, agree on a price, sign some documents, get your wire. Simple, right?

Each belief contains a kernel of truth. Advisory fees are real. You do know your business best. The process can seem straightforward on paper.

But I've interviewed dozens of founders who tried the DIY approach. They all tell the same story: lower valuations, worse terms, longer timelines, and deals that blow up at the finish line... and years of regret.

When your life's work is on the line, going solo isn't brave or financially prudent. It's reckless.

WHAT DIY FOUNDERS ALWAYS UNDERESTIMATE

The gap between perception and reality in exits is enormous. Here's what founders consistently underestimate:

The Information Asymmetry

Unless you've acquired multiple businesses yourself, you're sitting across from someone who has done dozens or hundreds of deals. They know exactly where the leverage points are, which terms matter, and how to spot weakness.

You're playing poker against a professional who can see your cards.

Sophisticated buyers have internal teams with thousands of hours of transaction experience. They recognise patterns you'll never see. They know which of your concerns are legitimate and which ones they can ignore.

* * * * * * * * * * * * * * * * * *

Sarah thought she'd won when she got the headline valuation she wanted for her agency. But she completely missed how the working capital adjustment was structured. It cost her over $700,000. The buyer knew exactly what they were doing, but Sarah only figured it out after the money was already gone.

The Technical Complexity

You've negotiated vendor contracts and employee deals. But exits involve deal structures, tax implications, and contractual details that can cost millions if you get them wrong.

Those legal terms that look like standard boilerplate? Some of them can come back to bite you years later. Earnout structures that sound generous? Often designed to pay out nothing.

The Psychological Minefield

Selling your business combines existential questions about your future with high-stakes financial decisions affecting your family's security.

Without advisors to share this burden, founders often crack under the pressure. Decision fatigue sets in. You start making concessions just to end the pain. The stress alone can cost you millions.

Your Advisory Dream Team: Who You Need and When

Selling your business isn't a solo sport – it's a team effort. So let's look at who should be on your exit team, and when to bring them in. Remember, the advisory team isn't just support – they're essential guides who've made this journey before and know the terrain intimately.

Still thinking you can do without? Think again.

The Opportunity Cost

While managing their own exits, founders must simultaneously run their businesses at peak performance. This divided attention typically leads to one of two outcomes: business performance suffers, or the exit process gets botched. Either way, the opportunity cost is substantial – and rarely factored into the "savings" of avoiding advisory fees.

The High Cost of No Advice

THE TAX DISASTER

Elena sold her marketing agency for $4.2 million, only to learn too late that parts of the deal were taxed as ordinary income, not capital gains. No tax advisor, no pre-exit structuring – just a $400,000 mistake she could have avoided with a single phone call.

THE EARNOUT TRAP

Ty thought he'd sold his business for $12 million: $8M upfront, $4M earnout. But the earnout metrics were tied to post-acquisition performance – metrics that became unachievable once folded into the acquirer's operations.

He ended up seeing less than $500,000 of that $4 million.

THE THREE ADVISORS YOU ACTUALLY NEED

You don't need a cast of thousands. You need the right people at the right time.

Your Board (Years Before Exit)

A strong board brings pattern recognition you can't get anywhere else. Board members who've successfully exited businesses see potential exit windows before you do, challenge your assumptions about value, and often have relationships with potential acquirers.

Most importantly, they keep you from falling in love with your own story. When you're ready to exit, that outside perspective becomes invaluable.

Kami (I was the 2nd largest non-founder individual investor) experienced a 2024 $300 million partial exit. A standing board agenda item was simply: "Exit"...? Timing, market conditions and energy were all regularly considered. When the time was right, the chair fronted these early conversations to keep the CEO focused on growth and out of the weeds. At the appropriate moment, the CEO and board stepped in to contribute and form an exit team.

Value-Building Advisor (2–3 Years Before Exit)

This is the person who will help you design an exit-ready business long before you're ready to sell. The transaction mechanics are only one piece of the puzzle – this is about building the kind of company buyers want to buy.

They help you reduce founder dependency, create scalable systems, and develop the narrative that will eventually become your exit story – and at this point in our journey, you'll hopefully recognise just how indispensable this skillset is. Think of them as your exit architect, designing the blueprint years before you need it.

Transaction Attorney (When You're Ready to Sell)

When you're negotiating a deal, you need someone who understands M&A law and can protect your interests. Your regular business lawyer won't cut it. This is specialised work involving representations, warranties, indemnifications, and deal structures that can haunt you for years if done wrong.

They're your insurance policy against the sophisticated legal teams on the other side.

Choosing the Right Advisors

Look for advisors with specific experience in your industry, company size, and likely buyer types. Generic experience rarely delivers the same value as specialists who understand your market dynamics. Interview them thoroughly, understand their fee structures upfront, and make sure the chemistry works. You'll be working closely with these people during one of the most stressful periods of your business life, so trust and communication matter as much as expertise.

WHY ADVISORS PAY FOR THEMSELVES

In busy industrial ports around the world, massive container ships worth hundreds of millions of dollars don't attempt to navigate into harbour alone. Even though the ship's captain has decades of experience and knows how to navigate, a local pilot flies out in a helicopter, drops onto the deck, and takes control for the final approach.

Why? Because the pilot knows every current, every hidden obstacle, every trick of that specific harbour. The captain knows how to sail. The pilot knows how to dock safely in these particular waters.

Your exit is your approach to harbour. **Professional advisors are your pilots.**

Still on the fence? Let's look at the numbers.

Professional representation typically increases exit values by 20–50% compared to DIY approaches. On a $15 million transaction, that could mean an additional $3–7.5 million in value compared to typical advisory fees of $300,000–$750,000.

Beyond headline valuation, advisors improve deal structure in ways that significantly impact what you receive. Better tax treatment, more favourable earnout terms, reduced escrow amounts. These structural improvements often add another 15–30% to your net proceeds.

Most importantly, professionally supported exits are far more likely to close. Based on my experience and industry conversations, DIY exits fail about 60–70% of the time. Professional exits fail about 20–30% of the time. The cost of a blown deal goes far beyond advisory fees: 6–12 months of wasted time, business disruption, and lost opportunity to exit during an optimal window.

WHEN YOUR BUSINESS IS ON FIRE

Red Adair had it exactly right: "If you think it's expensive to hire a professional, wait until you hire an amateur."

Your exit isn't the time to learn on the job. It's not the moment to discover what you don't know about information asymmetry, deal structures, or buyer psychology. It's definitely not when you want to find out that your "simple" transaction has blown up because of something you missed.

Most areas of life reward doing it yourself. Selling your business isn't one of them.

When the sum of all your blood, sweat and tears is on the line, don't bring a bucket of water to an oil fire. **Bring the professionals who know how to put it out.**

✔ CHECKPOINT: MORE IS LESS

- Are you tempted to handle your exit alone to "save" on advisory fees?
- Do you understand the three types of advisors you need and when to engage them?
- Have you considered what a failed DIY exit would cost you compared to professional fees?

CHAPTER 12

Don't Die in Due Diligence

"If you stay ready, you don't have to get ready."

– **Will Smith**

What skeletons would you rather find and fix yourself before a buyer does?

Due diligence is where good deals go to die – and where founders who aren't prepared often break under the pressure. It starts as a business evaluation, but feels intensely emotional and personal. Practically, it's an operational marathon that tests your resilience, transparency, and leadership under extreme conditions.

John's story is like so many others I know:

. . . .

"I thought we were already done. The LOI was signed. The price was agreed. We shook hands. Mentally, I'd already crossed the finish line.

Then due diligence started – and honestly, it nearly broke me.

We'd built the software business steadily, year after year, hitting $8 million in annual revenue over seven hard-fought years. The negotiations felt solid, and the strategic buyer clearly saw our value. I went home thinking the hard part was behind us. I'd done my job, now it was just paperwork, right?

I was totally wrong.

DD wasn't paperwork – it was like being interrogated. Endless, brutal document requests. Obscure emails at 2AM, demanding explanations for contracts I'd barely remembered signing years ago. Tense conference calls where my integrity was challenged over how we recognised revenue. And the gut-punch when they uncovered a technical vulnerability; something we'd consciously decided to push to next quarter.

Every day felt like a battle. Every question felt like an accusation. I stopped sleeping, stopped focusing clearly. The business suffered. My team felt the tension.

'How did I underestimate this so badly?'

That experience taught me one painful lesson I'll never forget:

Due diligence isn't paperwork. It's personal. It's relentless. It's the part of the exit that nobody warns you about – and the part that, if you're not careful, can cost you the entire deal."

This chapter reveals how to not just survive due diligence, but to use it as an opportunity to **strengthen your exit** and **protect what you've built.**

THE HIDDEN EMOTIONAL COST OF DUE DILIGENCE

Due diligence feels personal because, in many ways, it *is* personal. Your business isn't just a collection of assets and contracts – it's the manifestation of thousands of decisions you've made over the years. When buyers scrutinise those decisions, it feels like they're scrutinising **you**.

This creates (unanticipated) emotional challenges:

Identity Reckoning

Due diligence exposes something we talked about in Chapter 1: your business and your identity are tangled together. This is where that connection becomes brutally obvious.

When buyers question your technical architecture, they're questioning your technical judgment. When they scrutinise your financial decisions, they're evaluating your business acumen. When they analyse your team and structure, they're assessing your leadership.

* * * * * * * * * * * * * * * * * * * *

David, who had built his manufacturing company over fifteen years, described this phenomenon perfectly: "I never realised how much I defined myself by this business until strangers were questioning everything about it. Each document request felt like they were asking me to justify my worth as a human being, not just as a CEO."

This is why the emotional preparation we discussed in Chapter 1 – beginning to separate your identity from the business – becomes crucial during due diligence. Founders who have already started this psychological work are **significantly better equipped** to handle the scrutiny without defensive reactions or existential crises.

The Defensive Reflex

When buyers question your practices or decisions, the natural human reaction is defensiveness. This can show up as:

- Bristling at seemingly basic questions
- Providing unnecessarily elaborate justifications
- Taking criticism of the business as personal criticism
- Becoming argumentative rather than collaborative

One founder described becoming increasingly defensive when the buyer's team questioned her development methodology:

> *"They were questioning decisions we'd made years ago with limited resources and information. I had to keep reminding myself they weren't attacking me personally."*

The antidote: Remember that buyers aren't the enemy – they're doing their job of risk assessment.

Channel your inner **Closer** archetype: stay collaborative, answer directly, and *move forward*.

The Impostor Spiral

As due diligence uncovers inevitable issues or weaknesses, many founders experience impostor syndrome. The inner voice starts: "Maybe I'm not as good at this as I thought. What else have I been doing wrong? Will they discover I'm actually a fraud?"

A founder described this perfectly:

"Three weeks in, they found some customer contracts with non-standard terms I'd approved years earlier. It sent me into a spiral of self-doubt. If I'd missed this, what else was lurking? Was I actually a terrible CEO who just got lucky?"

The antidote: Go back to Chapter 1's work on separating your identity from your business. Every business has issues. *Perfect businesses don't exist.* Your job isn't to be flawless – it's to be transparent about what you've built. In his seminal book *Influence: The Psychology of Persuasion*, Robert Cialdini details the "Pratfall Effect", showing that openly admitting a small weakness or imperfection actually **builds trust and increases likability**. Fessing up creates credibility – and can add value to your deal.

The Exhaustion Factor

The sheer workload creates physical and mental fatigue that compounds everything else. You're managing regular business operations while responding to endless due diligence requests. Sleep deprivation from late nights preparing responses. Constant context-switching between operational and transaction issues.

One founder's health suffered significantly during a three-month due diligence period:

"I lost 12 pounds, developed insomnia, and had my first panic attack. All while trying to maintain a brave face for my team and family. Nobody warns you about the physical toll."

The antidote: This is where your advisory team from Chapter 11 becomes essential. Let them handle what they can handle, so you can focus on what only you can do.

UNDERSTANDING DUE DILIGENCE THROUGH THE BUYER LENS

As discussed in Chapter 5, different buyer types focus their due diligence on different priorities:

Strategic Buyers will dig deep into integration potential and synergies – scrutinising your technology stack, customer base, and market position to assess how smoothly you'll fit into their ecosystem.

Financial Buyers concentrate on predictability and risk – examining recurring revenue patterns, customer concentration, expense structures, and operational efficiency to build detailed return models.

Acquihire Buyers focus heavily on team dynamics and talent retention – analysing organisational structure, key personnel agreements, and cultural fit to ensure the talent they're buying will stay and thrive.

Succession Buyers emphasise operational maturity and transferability – reviewing documentation, processes, and leadership depth to confirm the business can run successfully without founder dependency.

Competitive Buyers take a strategic lens – examining market position, competitive advantages, and potential threats to understand how acquiring you changes the competitive landscape.

Knowing your buyer type from Chapter 5 helps you anticipate their specific due diligence focus and prepare accordingly.

Your practical Due Diligence Preparation Playbook (including the Data Room)

The best exits I've seen didn't treat due diligence as an afterthought – they started prepping 12 to 24 months out. Early prep reduces stress, protects your valuation, shortens timelines, and boosts close rates.

You'll find detailed checklists online, but here's the high-level structure most buyers expect:

1. FINANCIAL

- Clean, consistent financials reviewed by a pro.
- Clear metrics: customer concentration, retention, LTV, churn.
- Forecasts with assumptions and scenarios documented.

2. LEGAL & CONTRACTUAL

- All key contracts organised, especially change-of-control clauses.
- IP, employee, and contractor agreements locked down.
- Corporate structure and governance up-to-date.

3. OPERATIONAL

- Documented core processes and reporting lines.
- Evidence of customer satisfaction systems and data.
- Vendor lists and mitigation of key dependencies.

4. TECHNICAL

- Infrastructure, codebase, and roadmap documented.
- Security audits, compliance, and known technical debt addressed.

Don't see this as merely "exit preparation". It's simply great business hygiene. Founders who approach this proactively create ongoing value – whether they exit next year or in a decade. In reality, being surprised by buyer scrutiny during due diligence isn't bad luck; it's poor preparation. Proactively clean your house long before buyers arrive.

Operating at Peak While Under Scrutiny

One of the most challenging aspects of due diligence is maintaining business performance while managing the transaction process. Operational deterioration during due diligence can threaten the deal itself, creating a dangerous spiral where diligence findings lead to performance concerns, which lead to valuation adjustments.

When I was first approached about selling my very first business, I spoke to an investment banking mate, whose sage advice was: "Don't take your eye off the ball; keep growing your business."

So, first and foremost: keep running and growing your business exactly as you always have. Don't abandon your standard playbook or change what's been working. The suggestions below are additions to your normal operations, not replacements for them.

Divide and Conquer

You can't do everything. Read that twice. Split responsibilities clearly: designate specific team members to lead due diligence responses while others maintain focus on core business operations. Define who makes what decisions and when to escalate.

Tom made a smart division when his company entered

due diligence. His CFO and head of legal handled most buyer requests while he and his COO kept the business running. When buyers needed technical deep-dives, they pulled in the CTO but protected the engineering team from constant disruption.

Control the Information Flow

The tension between transparency and confidentiality creates real challenges. Decide early which team members need to know about the transaction. Develop standard responses for unusual activities. "We're working with consultants on some strategic planning" usually works.

Shield Your Team

Your team's performance directly impacts business results during this critical period. Create buffers to minimise disruption from buyer requests. Maintain normal rhythms and routines. Watch closely for signs of stress or burnout.

Lisa maintained her weekly team meetings and regular one-on-ones throughout the process, creating a sense of normalcy despite the chaos happening behind the scenes.

Don't Forget Your Customers

Customer relationships can easily suffer when you're distracted. Stay vigilant about service quality. If buyers want customer references, contact each reference first to provide context while maintaining confidentiality about the transaction.

SURVIVAL GUIDE: MANAGING THE EMOTIONAL TOLL

Due diligence will feel **personal, intrusive,** and occasionally **adversarial.** This isn't because buyers are trying to be difficult – they're doing their job of risk assessment on a major investment. A few strategies that help:

- **Set realistic expectations.** Know in advance it's going to be brutal. Every business has issues. Perfection isn't the goal, but candour is. Be transparent about what you've built.

- **Create emotional distance.** Separate your identity from your business (remember Chapter 1!). Questions about the business *aren't automatically judgments about your character.*

- **Build in recovery time.** One founder made it through by going surfing every Wednesday evening, regardless of what was happening with the deal. For those few hours, he couldn't check email or take calls. He returned with better perspective and emotional stability. Find something that works for you... *and stick to it.*

- **Use your advisory team.** This is exactly why you have the support system from Chapter 11. Let them handle what they can handle.

Looking Ahead: The Integration Bridge

Due diligence isn't the final hurdle – it's actually the beginning of integration (which we'll explore in Chapter 13). The questions buyers ask during diligence directly shape their integration plans.

Smart founders recognise this connection. When buyers scrutinise your technology, they're identifying integration

Hiding issues might get you through closing, but it creates much bigger problems when reality emerges post-acquisition.

challenges. When they analyse your team structure, they're planning organisational changes. When they examine customer contracts, they're developing retention strategies.

This is why transparency during diligence **directly impacts integration success.**

Hiding issues might get you through closing, but it creates much bigger problems when reality emerges post-acquisition.

The best founders view diligence not as something to "get through", but as the foundation for successful integration – the beginning of the relationship that will determine their legacy and their team's future.

Remember: Due diligence isn't just a transaction requirement – it's a test of your preparation, transparency, and resilience under pressure. The founders who navigate it most successfully are those who prepare thoroughly, respond constructively to inevitable issues, and maintain perspective throughout the process.

With proper preparation and the right mindset, due diligence becomes not just survivable, but an opportunity to demonstrate the quality of what you've built. And to ensure that the transaction truly captures the value you've created.

Winning through due diligence is a great battle. Once the deal closes and the champagne goes flat, the next phase of work begins. How you navigate integration will determine whether your exit delivers on its full promise – protecting what you've built while **unlocking the growth you envisioned.**

✔ FINAL CHECKPOINT FOR PART III
THINK YOU'RE READY? LET'S FIND OUT.

- Are your financials, legal contracts, strategy, and reporting up-to-date for deep buyer scrutiny?
- Have you role-played intense, potentially uncomfortable questions about your business decisions?
- Have you engaged advisors to help you understand what buyers will examine during due diligence?
- Do you have your operating rhythm and team roles clearly defined to continue performing at peak during the process?
- Have you identified potential red flags or areas of concern that might emerge, and developed plans to address them?

PART III CONCLUSION:
POWER FROM PREPARATION

Like a band that toils, practices and suffers for years before the overnight success breakthrough, **great exits aren't accidents.** They're the culmination of considered preparation, clever positioning, and the insight to move when the timing is right.

Seneca was right when he described luck as preparedness meeting opportunity. To truly know your archetype, your great question to answer is:

"What exit do I truly seek?"

Your great opportunity is to prepare your business to look the best it can for the right acquirer, and then understand competitive tension building.

The gap between building a business and selling one is bigger than most founders realise. Building rewards your ability to figure things out as you go, to trust your gut, to move fast and break things.

Selling is different. It rewards methodical preparation, professional guidance, and the emotional discipline to stay rational when strangers are questioning every decision you've made over the past decade.

Don't show up to a gun fight with a knife. Winning the exit requires playing a different game.

Which brings us to the final piece of the puzzle: getting the deal done **without losing what matters most...**

> *"The truth doesn't mind being questioned.*
> *Lies do."*
>
> – Unknown

PART IV

The Legacy Dimension

ENGINEERING YOUR NEXT CHAPTER

The deal is a drop. The legacy is the sea it falls into.

CHAPTER 13

The Integration Trap

"The most dangerous phase of any mission is re-entry."

– NASA principle

How will you measure success a year from now – by the size of the cheque, or by what's left behind?

Closing day feels like victory. After months of due diligence, negotiations, and sleepless nights, you've successfully sold your business.

The wire has hit your account.

Your team is celebrating.

You should be proud – this is a massive achievement.

But the story isn't over.

The next epoch in your journey, **integration,** will shape your legacy, your team's future, and whether the vision that drove your exit becomes reality.

. . . .

Remember AOL-Time Warner in 2000? They called it creating a media powerhouse. Now it's remembered as the biggest value-destroying merger in corporate history. Cultural clashes and strategic missteps unravelled the combined company,

wiping out over $200 billion in shareholder value (basically New Zealand's entire annual GDP gone for a year!).
All because they nailed the deal but botched the integration.

This chapter shows you what happens after the deal closes: how to spot integration challenges before they hit, and how to protect what matters most.

Integration is when the buyer takes your carefully built business and starts reshaping it – combining teams, merging products, aligning cultures, and chasing those promised "synergies".

Get it right, and integration unlocks extraordinary value for everyone.

Get it wrong, and years of careful work can unravel in months.

INTEGRATION: THE FORGOTTEN DEAL KILLER

More than half of all acquisitions fail to meet their intended goals – not because the deal was flawed, but because the integration failed.

The numbers tell the story:

- Between 70-90% of acquisitions fail to deliver their expected value, primarily due to integration challenges[3]
- Around 30% of acquired employees leave within the first year post-acquisition[4]
- Earnouts tied to business performance are achieved in full less than 20% of the time[5]
- Customer retention often drops 15-30% in the two years following an acquisition[6]

The most heart-breaking stories I've encountered aren't

about bad acquirers. They're about great companies acquired by good buyers, but are then destroyed by disastrous integrations.

In 2012, Google acquired Motorola Mobility for $12.5 billion, aiming to combine Motorola's hardware expertise with Google's software innovation and to strengthen Android's patent portfolio. However, integration challenges quickly emerged. Motorola's traditional, hardware-focused culture clashed with Google's fast-paced, software-driven environment, leading to significant leadership turnover and a sharp decline in employee morale. Although Google released new devices like the Moto X and Moto G, these products struggled to gain traction in a competitive market, hindered by weak distribution and unclear positioning.

Customer dissatisfaction grew as promised handset upgrades failed to materialise, damaging Motorola's brand loyalty. Financial losses mounted, with Motorola bleeding hundreds of millions each quarter. Less than two years later, Google sold Motorola to Lenovo at a $9 billion markdown, retaining only select patents and a small R&D team.

A high-profile reminder that poor integration can undermine even the most promising deals. Understanding why these integrations fail starts with seeing the process through the buyer's eyes. I know it's a hard pill to swallow, but they're not trying to preserve what you built – they're trying to extract maximum value from what they bought.

UNDERSTANDING THE BUYER'S PERSPECTIVE

To avoid integration nightmares, you need to clearly understand how buyers approach integration.

Buyers typically choose one of three paths:

Absorption: Your company disappears into theirs completely – branding, products, culture, teams. Maximum integration, maximum risk.

Standalone Subsidiary: Your business continues largely as-is, with minimal integration. Lower risk, but less synergy.

Hybrid Integration: Parts of your company remain independent (often product or tech), while other areas (HR, sales, operations) integrate fully.

Each approach has clear pros and cons. The danger isn't the approach itself; it's misunderstanding or misalignment between your expectations and the buyer's strategy. From a buyer's perspective, integration isn't about preserving what you've built – it's about extracting every dollar of value they paid for. That means:

They're looking to cut costs wherever they can duplicate what you do. Why pay for two finance teams, two HR departments, two office leases? Your carefully chosen systems, your preferred vendors, your way of doing things – all potentially on the chopping block if they have their own version. That expensive office space you fought to get in the perfect location? It might be gone in six months.

They want to make money from what you've built. Your customer list becomes their cross-sell opportunity. Your product becomes part of their bundle. Your distribution channels become their expansion path. Every relationship you've spent years nurturing suddenly becomes part of their growth strategy.

They want everyone rowing in the same direction. Your

flat startup culture might clash with their corporate hierarchy. Your rapid decision-making process might be slowed to match their approval processes. The scrappy, move-fast mentality that got you here? That might not fit their playbook.

THE OPERATIONAL REALITY OF INTEGRATION

Here's what integration actually looks like when you're living through it:

Your team structure gets turned upside down. People who used to report to you now report to someone you've never met. Your head of sales suddenly has a new boss in another country. That tight-knit leadership team that made decisions over coffee? Now every choice goes through three layers of approval. The org chart you spent years perfecting gets redrawn by people who've never worked a day in your business. This is where it gets brutal.

Your product roadmap becomes someone else's priority list. Features your customers have been begging for get deprioritised because they don't fit the buyer's master plan. Your elegant tech stack gets forced into their legacy systems. The innovative approach that differentiated you in the market? Shelved because it doesn't align with their platform strategy.

Then comes the process overhaul. Remember that streamlined vendor you loved working with? They'll be gone – replaced with their enterprise contract that takes three weeks to get a simple change approved. Your five-minute customer support fixes now require formal tickets and escalation procedures. Everything that made you fast and nimble gets wrapped in their corporate red tape. The 95% customer satisfaction scores you were proud of? Those start sliding as your personal touch gets "standardised" into their playbook.

Your customer relationships get "managed". Communication that used to come directly from you now gets filtered through their customer success team. Pricing conversations move from handshake deals to formal contracts that require legal approval. The personal relationships you spent years building become "accounts" in their CRM system. Your customers start asking where you went, and you realise you're no longer allowed to talk to them directly without going through proper channels.

This might sound inevitable – and it certainly sounds as fun as cutting your toenails with a chainsaw – but it doesn't have to be. Because smart founders turn integration planning into their **biggest advantage.**

FLIP THE INTEGRATION SCRIPT

Integration planning feels defensive, but it's your best offensive weapon. Done right, you'll improve your terms, create buyer tension, and still protect what matters most.

Don't Let Them Set All the Rules

Instead of waiting for buyers to tell you how integration will work, **show up with your own plan.** When you walk into that meeting with a clear 90-day framework already mapped out, you're taking control of the conversation. You're showing them you understand the risks better than they do, elevating your status in the deal. It also helps them appreciate that this isn't going to be a simple "absorb and move on" situation.

Make Them Sweat a Little

Buyers get nervous when it clicks that you're not desperate. Keep your other options visible. Just like we discussed in

Chapter 7, talk to multiple buyers – and make sure they know it. Show them you've thought through what happens if integration goes wrong and what it'll cost them. The moment they think you might walk away over integration terms, their whole approach changes. Suddenly, they're asking what you need instead of telling you what they're going to do.

Protect Your People by Protecting Their Money

Don't ask for team protections as favours – show how losing key people will cost them real revenue. When you can demonstrate that disrupting your customer success team puts $2M of ARR at risk, your "team protection requirements" become their financial safeguards. Frame everything in terms of protecting their investment, not your preferences.

Show Them You're Not Amateur Hour

Buyers love dealing with naïve founders who haven't thought past the cheque clearing. They can dictate terms, control the process, and integrate however they want because the founder is just grateful someone wrote them said cheque.

Don't be that founder.

Show up with documentation they haven't even thought to ask for yet. Have customer communication templates ready for the acquisition announcement. Build integration dashboards before they mention wanting to track metrics. Create knowledge transfer protocols for your key roles before they realise they need them.

When you're that prepared, two things happen. First, they realise you're not going to be an easy integration where they can just absorb your business and move on. Second, they start wondering what other buyers you're talking to who've helped you get this sophisticated.

The most powerful signal you can send is that you've done this dance before – or at least thought deeply about every step. Buyers expect founders to be operationally strong but strategically naïve about exits. When you prove you're neither, the entire dynamic shifts.

They stop treating you like someone who needs their help and start treating you like **someone they need to win over**. That's exactly where you want to be when integration terms hit the table.

Navigating Earn-outs and Integration Risk

Here's the nightmare scenario: you sign an earnout thinking you're in control of hitting your targets, then watch helplessly as their integration decisions make those targets impossible to reach.

If part of your valuation involves an earnout, integration risk doesn't just multiply – it becomes an existential threat to getting paid what you're owed. Buyers can unintentionally (or very intentionally) damage your earnout potential through integration decisions that seem reasonable to them, but kill your performance.

The problem is simple: earnouts assume you'll keep operating roughly the same way you always have. But integration means everything changes.

- Your sales team gets new managers who don't understand your customers.
- Your marketing budget gets reallocated to fit their corporate priorities.
- Your product roadmap gets shifted to align with their platform strategy.

Getting integration right isn't luck
– it's preparation.

Suddenly, those revenue targets that seemed totally achievable become impossible.

Make sure you can control the things they're measuring you on. If your earnout is tied to revenue growth, you need decision rights over sales, marketing, and pricing. If it's tied to product milestones, you need protection against technology changes that derail your roadmap. If it's tied to customer retention, you need guarantees about service levels and support quality.

Don't just negotiate the metrics – **negotiate what happens when they change the game.** Build in adjustment mechanisms for when their integration decisions impact your performance. Include acceleration provisions that pay you out early if certain integration milestones trigger. Most importantly, create clear accounting separation so their financial reporting changes don't suddenly make your numbers look different.

The smart money is on engineering your earnout structure for protection and fairness before you need it, because once integration starts, **it's too late to renegotiate.**

Getting integration right isn't luck – it's preparation.

The founders who come out of integration with their businesses intact, their teams happy, and their earnouts paid aren't the ones who hoped for the best. They're the ones who **planned for the worst** and **negotiated for what mattered most.**

✔ CHECKPOINT: HAVE YOU INVESTED IN INTEGRATION?

- Do you truly understand exactly how your buyer intends to handle your business post-sale?
- What protections have you negotiated around team retention, cultural integrity, and operational independence?
- Are your earn-out structures clearly protected from negative integration outcomes?
- Have you proactively prepared and communicated openly with your team about integration realities and expectations?
- Have you documented integration plans and expectations as part of your deal process?

Integration isn't a post-sale detail – it's the final, critical chapter of your exit. Treat it with the strategic clarity and proactive planning it deserves.

Your exit isn't done when you close the deal. It's only truly complete when your business successfully integrates and your legacy endures.

Make integration your strength, not your nightmare.

CHAPTER 14

The Wealth Paradox

*"The pursuit of wealth is a great servant
and a terrible master."*

– Tim Ferriss

*"Success is getting what you want.
Happiness is wanting what you get."*

– Dale Carnegie

Do you want the money you dreamed of to leave you feeling empty? Here's how to avoid it.

THE WEALTH LEARNING CURVE

For years, you mastered the art of making money. Every dollar that came into your business had a purpose – payroll, growth, inventory, marketing. You could tell me exactly where every cent was going and why. You were (probably) a cash flow ninja.

Now you have to learn the completely different skill of **having** money.

> *No amount of business success prepares you for the psychological reality of having a very large sum sitting in your account with no clear monthly rhythm attached to it.*

And nobody prepared you for how totally different those skills are.

The Windfall Mindfuck

There's a psychological difference between making money gradually and receiving a massive lump sum all at once – even when you've earned every penny of it.

When someone wins more than $10 million in the lottery, 78% of winners lose it all within five years. When someone receives millions from an insurance settlement, they often wake up thinking, "I've got this money, but nothing's actually changed." And when you sell your company for eight or nine figures? You stare at that bank balance feeling both infinite and terrifyingly finite at the same time.

The difference isn't about earning versus luck – it's about **scale** and **suddenness.** You've spent years managing hundreds of thousands, maybe millions in business cash flow. Now you're looking at generational wealth that arrived in a single transfer.

Your brain, which was wired for "revenue in, expenses out,

repeat monthly", suddenly has to process a number so large it breaks your normal financial frameworks. The psychological impact of sudden scale – even earned scale – creates the same disorientation that lottery winners experience.

The problem isn't that you didn't earn it. The problem is that no amount of business success prepares you for the psychological reality of having a very large sum sitting in your account with no clear monthly rhythm attached to it.

The Halo Effect Risk

Here's what happens. You sell your company for big money, and suddenly you think you're Warren Buffett. After all, you built something valuable from nothing – surely you can pick winning investments, develop profitable real estate, or spot the next big startup?

Building a company and deploying capital are completely different games with completely different rules. Your founder superpowers don't transfer. The decisiveness that served you well becomes recklessness when you're writing six-figure cheques to startups you barely understand. The risk tolerance that built your business becomes the thing that destroys your wealth.

As one Wealth Manager puts it: "I've seen people who've been very successful in one type of business think the same characteristics that worked there would work in a totally different business. It sounded good in theory, but the two just didn't work."

The Monthly Income Paradigm Shift

Then there's the psychological weirdness of having a massive lump sum instead of regular income. For years, money came in monthly – revenue, salary, whatever. You had a rhythm. Cash in, cash out, repeat. Your brain learned to think in monthly cycles.

Now you're staring at one huge number in your account, and your brain has no framework for it. Do you live off it? Invest it all? Spend some? How much is "some"?

Lottery winners encapsulate this perfectly: they feel both rich and broke simultaneously. They have millions but no "salary" anymore. Your nervous system doesn't know how to process abundance when it's been trained for scarcity and monthly cash management. The founders who navigate this successfully take time, make a plan, and recognise that the skills that *made* you wealthy are different from the skills needed to *keep* you wealthy.

THE NEW SOCIAL DYNAMICS

The moment word gets out about your exit, every relationship in your life shifts. And I mean every single one. I know how this sounds – kinda like complaining about people wanting to share in your success. But the isolation and confusion are real, and understanding these dynamics helps you navigate them better.

Unfortunately, everyone wants something

It starts subtly. Old friends reaching out after years of silence. Extended family members suddenly remembering your birthday. Former colleagues suggesting coffee to "catch up".

Then it gets less subtle. The investment opportunities start flowing. Your brother-in-law's brilliant business idea that just needs a small injection of capital. The charity galas where you're suddenly the perfect person to sponsor a table. Everyone has something they're sure you'd love to be involved in.

What's most difficult is that you can't tell who's genuine anymore. That friend who suggests dinner – are they actually happy for you, or do they have a pitch coming? Your cousin who's been texting more – do they care about your success, or are they thinking about their mortgage?

Friends and family: when relationships get complicated

You become the rich friend, and rich friends are often lonely friends.

Suddenly you're paying for every dinner because "you can afford it". Planning trips becomes awkward because your idea of a vacation and their idea of a vacation are now completely different price points. You suggest a restaurant, and everyone goes quiet because they're calculating if *they* can afford it.

You start feeling guilty about everything.

Guilty for suggesting the nice place. Guilty for not suggesting the nice place. Guilty for paying. Guilty for not paying. You're walking on eggshells in relationships that used to be effortless.

Family dynamics can be even more complex. Some families rally around success – they're genuinely proud and supportive. But others see dollar signs and suddenly have opinions about how you should be spending "your" money on "family".

The questions start.

- *What about college funds for the kids?*
- *Shouldn't you help pay off your parents' mortgage?*
- *Your sister's struggling with her business – surely you could help out?*
- *The family vacation this year should be somewhere nice now that you can afford it, right?*

Money doesn't just change your bank balance. It changes how the world sees you and interacts with you. And that shift is often more disorienting than the wealth itself.

Then there are the inheritance conversations that haven't even happened yet, but somehow everyone's thinking about. The power dynamics shift. Family members who used to treat you as an equal might suddenly either defer to you or resent you.

Many exited founders stop talking to their old friends and limit family interactions because every conversation feels transactional. Either you're the ATM or you're the asshole who won't help out.

The sympathy vacuum

Perhaps the cruellest irony is that you can't complain about any of this without sounding like an entitled prick. Try explaining to anyone that having millions of dollars is psychologically difficult and watch their eyes roll. "Boohoo for you, you've got $20 million. I've got real problems like paying my mortgage."

So you suffer in silence. The isolation, the relationship strain, the constant second-guessing of people's motives – none of it gets acknowledged because **you're supposed to be grateful and happy.**

Money doesn't just change your bank balance. It changes

how the world sees you and interacts with you. And that shift is often more disorienting than the wealth itself.

SETTING BOUNDARIES EARLY

The founders who navigate this best are proactive about these conversations. They set clear expectations early, decide in advance what they're comfortable contributing to family and causes, and communicate those boundaries before awkward requests arise.

It's easier to say "I've allocated X amount annually for family assistance" than to evaluate each request in the moment while feeling guilty. This keeps the emotional honesty while adding practical value and acknowledging that not all wealthy people's problems deserve sympathy – but understanding them helps you prepare.

THE GENERATIONAL WEIGHT

You used to worry about your business. Now you worry about your bloodline.

The math is simple but terrifying: if you don't completely screw this up, this money could last for generations. But that also means if you do screw it up, you're not just losing your own financial security – you're potentially destroying your family's future for decades.

Every decision becomes a referendum on your competence as a wealth steward. The money sits there while you research and re-research every possible scenario, terrified of making the wrong choice.

LEARNING WHAT ACTUALLY WORKS

Having real money means you can afford to make mistakes and figure out what actually brings you satisfaction. This experimentation phase is normal and valuable. You're not failing at being rich – you're learning what rich means for *you specifically*.

I went through this same process after my first exit. I looked around for new expensive hobbies and collections, thinking I needed to find something "worthy" of my new financial situation.

But when I really paid attention to where my money wanted to go, it was the same place it had always gone – toward art. I'd been buying art since I was eight years old, just at different price points as my situation changed. The joy wasn't in discovering some new rich person hobby. It was in being able to pursue what had always interested me, just without the financial constraints.

Founders typically follow a similar pattern. Maybe the boat was a waste, but the flying lessons weren't. Maybe the expensive art collection doesn't move you, but funding that documentary project does. You try things, learn what resonates, and gradually figure out where your money wants to go.

The founders who find a genuine sense of contentment and purpose eventually stop trying to buy happiness and start using their wealth as a tool to create the *conditions* for happiness – deeper connections, unique experiences, meaningful projects.

The truth is simpler and more liberating than you think: money buys you *options*, not happiness. The satisfaction comes from what you *do* with those options, not from having them.

And what brings satisfaction is deeply personal – it can't be purchased from a luxury catalogue or found on a "things rich people buy" list.

The expensive stuff isn't the point. **It never was.** The point is having the freedom to discover what actually matters to you and the resources to pursue it.

THE INVESTMENT MINEFIELD

The withdrawal symptoms hit about six months after your exit. You miss the adrenaline of building something. You miss being needed, making decisions that matter, seeing your vision come to life. The money is nice, but it's not scratching the itch that drove you for years.

Then a founder pitches you their startup, and **something inside you lights up again.**

Angel investing feels like the perfect solution. You get to be involved in building again without the full-time commitment. You understand the founder's journey better than anyone. You can add real value beyond just money. Plus, you built something successful – surely you can spot other winners, right?

This is where **emotional need meets dangerous psychology.**

THE SKILLS DON'T TRANSFER

Building a company and picking companies are completely different skills. As a founder, you had deep knowledge of one market, one customer base, one set of problems. As an investor, you're trying to evaluate dozens of different markets, business models, and founders across industries you may know nothing about.

The same decisiveness and risk tolerance that served you well as a founder become liabilities when managing significant capital without the guardrails your business provided.

THE BIG MONEY MISTAKE

You have millions sitting in your account. A $100,000 or $200,000 investment feels reasonable – it's a tiny percentage of your net worth. But you're skipping the learning curve that every successful angel investor goes through.

Smart investors start with $5,000 or $10,000 cheques. They make mistakes, learn from them, and gradually increase investments as they develop pattern recognition. You're jumping straight to the scale that could fund someone's entire angel portfolio.

The math is brutal: if you write ten $200,000 cheques and eight fail completely (they will), you've just lost $1,600,000 learning lessons that could have cost you $20,000.

THE PATH FORWARD

The founders who become successful angel investors treat it like any other skill: they start small, learn constantly, and **build up slowly**. Most importantly, they separate their need to stay involved in building from their investment strategy. The investment opportunities *will always be there*. Your exit money won't come back if you blow it trying to recreate the high of building something from nothing.

What now?

So you've learned to manage the social dynamics of wealth, figured out what spending actually satisfies you, and avoided blowing your money on bad investments. You've handled the practical challenges of sudden wealth.

Next is what founders almost always discover: even when you get all of this right, there's still a bigger question waiting.

What's it all for?

The founders who find true fulfilment post-exit realise that wealth isn't the end of their journey – it's the beginning of a more meaningful chapter. The same elements that created meaning before wealth continue to create meaning after it: deep relationships, meaningful contribution, personal growth, and experiences that matter.

The question isn't how to enjoy your money. It's how to use your freedom and resources to create something that outlasts you.

✔ CHECKPOINT: WEALTH IS MORE THAN THE WIRE

- Pre-exit: What aspects of sudden wealth are you most concerned about?
- Post-exit: What aspects have caught you most off guard?
- How might your relationships change after an exit, and which ones are you most worried about? What boundaries might you need to set?
- What does your current spending tell you about your values?
- Where might you be most vulnerable to making expensive mistakes with wealth, and what safeguards could you put in place?
- Beyond managing money effectively, what deeper purpose do you want your wealth to serve?

Remember: The wealth from your exit is necessary, but *not sufficient for genuine fulfilment.* Money provides freedom from financial constraints, but freedom without direction is just expensive confusion.

The wire transfer will never fulfil you. Only the purpose behind how you use that wealth can.

The question every wealthy founder eventually faces isn't *"How do I manage my money?".* It's *"What am I supposed to do with my life now?".* That question – and how to answer it – is where your real post-exit journey begins.

> *"There are a great many people accumulating what they think is vast wealth, but it's only money."*
>
> – Alan Watts

CHAPTER 15

When Achievement Starts Sucking

"Achievement has no value if it robs you of joy."

– Robin Sharma

. . . .

Do you need to be doing this, my love?"

My girlfriend Tina was standing behind my desk chair, her hand on my shoulder, watching me sit hunched over like Rodin's Thinker. Except I wasn't pondering the mysteries of existence. I was just hurting.

It was a Wednesday in 2019, and I was supposedly "living the dream". Three years into our AI platform startup Ambit, several million dollars raised, well into seven figures of recurring revenue. I had a full plate as Founder, CEO and Chair, and we'd moved from Auckland to Sydney to ride what everyone expected would be continued stratospheric growth.

Except we'd stalled. Badly.

I was the squeeze point between sales, customers, partners, staff, board, investors, and co-founders. I'd just survived a "please explain" meeting with investors, two performance *management conversations, a board meeting focused on finding leaks, and a blow-up with a difficult co-founder. All in one day.*

I was working from home, forehead in hand, flirting with burnout and miserable, when Tina asked that question.

It was exactly what I needed to hear.

THE TRAP I DIDN'T SEE COMING

Her question sent my mind racing back to why I'd started **Ambit** in the first place. Not the pitch deck reasons or the market opportunity bullshit. The *real* reasons.

I wanted to build something exciting from the ground up. I wanted to guide early growth and watch something come alive. I already had money from my previous exits, so this wasn't about needing the cash. And I specifically didn't want endless travel, politics, or being beholden to other people's priorities.

I'd forgotten every single one of these things.

Here's what I learned sitting at that desk: **having money doesn't make you immune to chasing the wrong things.** Even when you don't need the revenue, even when you've already proven you can build and exit successfully, it's incredibly easy to get caught up in the metrics instead of the meaning.

I got caught up in the game. Made other people's priorities my own. Started measuring success by monthly recurring revenue and investor sentiment instead of whether I was building something I cared about.

That's the trap founders often never see coming after a successful exit. You think having "enough" money protects you from making decisions based on money. **It doesn't.** The scoreboard is seductive, no matter how much you already have.

There's a deeper issue at play: when your life fundamentally

I needed to consciously choose what success meant now that the game had changed.

changes – financial freedom achieved, business constraints removed – you need to consciously choose new values to guide your decisions. Most founders never do this recalibration. We keep operating from the value system that got us there: **achievement at any cost, growth above all else, revenue as validation.**

These values made sense when survival was on the line. They're poison when you already have everything you need.

That question from Tina forced me to accelerate my succession plan and immediately reduce my hours. **Life improved immediately.** But it also forced me to confront something I'd never considered:

I needed to consciously choose what success meant now that the game had changed.

THE VALUES AUDIT

Most people have never actually examined the values driving their decisions. It's hard work. It's reflective. And when we do attempt it, we often consider the values we'd like to have rather than the ones we're making decisions from.

Even if you've done this work before, chances are you haven't revisited it in years. Values change as life changes, but we keep operating from outdated frameworks without realising it.

Want proof? Think back to the critical decisions you made ten years ago. What mattered to you then? What were you optimising for? Now compare that to what drives your decisions today. Different, right? Your circumstances changed, your priorities shifted, but did you ever consciously update your decision-making framework?

For founders, this values drift happens in fast forward. We inherit startup values – growth at any cost, revenue as validation, market dominance as the goal. These values work when you're fighting for survival, trying to prove your business model, or simply keeping the lights on.

But when you've already won that game? When financial pressure is gone and you have the luxury of choice? Operating from those same values becomes a prison.

I was making **Ambit** decisions based on values from my first startup: when I was broke, unproven, and desperately needed external validation. By the time Tina asked that question, I had financial freedom and a track record. I could optimise for personal satisfaction, team culture, or building something I genuinely cared about.

But I was still keeping score like a first-time founder with everything to prove.

Most successful people resist values recalibration because it's hard, it feels like we're giving up our competitive edge and probably most importantly – we've trained ourselves to be achievement machines. Changing the game feels like weakness.

It's not weakness. It's evolution.

RECALIBRATING YOUR VALUES

A deep journaling exercise spread over several weeks and multiple sessions served me incredibly well. My observation is that most avoid this work because it feels overwhelming or too introspective, but it's some of the most practical work you can do after achieving financial freedom.

The process isn't quick, and it shouldn't be. You're examining decision-making patterns you've relied on for years, and rewiring them takes time. I found that spreading the work across a few sessions over several weeks gave me space to process between sessions rather than trying to force insights.

There are different ways to approach this work, depending on how your mind naturally operates:

Some people find it revealing to examine the **gap between their stated values and actual behaviours** – what does your calendar really show you prioritise versus what you say matters most?

Others prefer looking at **life seasons** – recognising that the values serving you in your building phase might be different from what serves you now.

A third approach focuses on **energy** – what activities and decisions consistently energise you versus drain you, and working backward to understand the underlying values.

There's also the straightforward **past, present, future** reflection – understanding what values drove your business journey, what's driving you now, and what you want to optimise for going forward.

Interestingly, I've noticed that the different exit archetypes from Chapter 8 tend to gravitate toward different approaches. **Maximisers** often prefer the behavioural analysis; **Legacy**

Builders connect with the life seasons framework; **Closers** like the energy-based approach; **Equity Earners** appreciate the systematic past-present-future method. But there's no right or wrong choice – pick whatever aligns with how your brain ticks over.

The key insight I discovered:

Your values should evolve as your life evolves.

The values that got you to financial freedom aren't necessarily the ones that will get you to a true sense of inner harmony, contentment, and overall satisfaction. But most of us never consciously make that transition.

This isn't weekend work. The people who rush this process usually end up recreating the same patterns in new contexts. But when you do the work properly, it changes everything about how you make decisions.

I'll give you detailed questions for each approach in the checkpoint section at the end of this chapter.

WHAT CARNEGIE FIGURED OUT

The Achievement Addiction

Many founders discover they're addicted to the building process itself – the adrenaline of problems that need solving, teams that need leading, mountains that need climbing. But they keep chasing achievement metrics even when achievement isn't what they need anymore. The addiction is real. The metrics are just the drug.

Andrew Carnegie understood this better than almost anyone in history. He built Carnegie Steel and sold it in 1901 for what would be about $300 billion in today's money. But Carnegie didn't spend the next 20 years counting his cash or trying to make more.

He spent it giving every penny away.

Carnegie built over 2,500 libraries worldwide and funded universities that are still changing lives today. Ask anyone what Carnegie's greatest accomplishment was, and they won't mention the steel company. They'll talk about the libraries that educated millions of people who never could have afforded books otherwise.

From Legacy to Impact

Carnegie wasn't thinking about legacy – what he'd leave behind. He was thinking about impact – what he could set in motion. And he figured out that his post-exit superpower wasn't the money itself, but the rare combination of skills he'd developed: systematic thinking, resource deployment, and the ability to create lasting institutions.

But only because he consciously chose new values to guide those capabilities.

Carnegie made the shift from measuring success by what he could accumulate to measuring success by what he could transform. From building wealth to creating impact and from personal achievement to a contribution that would outlast him.

The founders I know who found genuine fulfilment after their exits made the same shift.

In a terrifyingly short time, your exit number will be forgotten. Even by you. **What you do with the freedom and resources it gives you won't be.**

YOUR TURN

Sure, Carnegie had certain advantages – different era, unprecedented wealth, fewer distractions. But the fundamental principle applies whether you have $10 million or $300 billion: once you have enough money to cover your needs, the real work begins. Sorry for getting all Ram Dass on you, but it's something you need to hear.

The exercises that follow are designed around the four approaches we discussed. Pick the one that feels most natural to how you process information, then commit to doing the work properly over several weeks.

This is the foundation for everything that comes next.

VALUES RECALIBRATION EXERCISES

Approach 1: Values vs. Behaviours Gap

Tends to appeal to Maximisers who prefer data-driven analysis using behavioural economics principles –examining the gap between stated preferences and revealed preferences through actual choices.

Past Behaviours (Weeks 1-2):

- Review your calendar from the 6 months before you started thinking about exit/transition. What does your time allocation reveal about your actual priorities?

- Review big-ticket spending items over the past year (beyond necessities). What do these choices say about your values?

- List your last 5 significant decisions, categorised as: Business/Career, Personal/Family, Financial/Investment. What criteria drove each decision?

Stated Values (Weeks 3-4):

- Identify and list your top 5 values.
- For each stated value, find 2 specific examples from the past year where your actions reflected this value.
- Where you can't find examples, ask: Why do you think this value matters if you're not acting on it?

Gaps and Redesign (Weeks 5-6):

- Where are the biggest gaps between stated and lived values? What's driving those gaps?
- Which current behaviours serve outdated values from your survival/building phase?
- If you could only measure success by 3 metrics going forward, what would they be?

Approach 2: Life Seasons Framework

Tends to appeal to Legacy Builders who think in long-term contribution arcs.

This approach is adapted from the Hindu concept of life's four stages (ashramas) for the modern founder journey.

Learn Season (Weeks 1-2):

- What were your core values during your early career/learning phase? Write them down specifically.
- What external pressures shaped those values? (Proving yourself, gaining experience, building credibility?)

- Which of those early values served you well? Which ones evolved as you gained experience?

Earn Season (Weeks 3-4):

- What did "winning" mean to you during your peak wealth-building years?
- When you had to choose between personal values and business success, which typically won and why?
- What did you sacrifice or compromise during your earning season that you want to reclaim?

Return Season (Weeks 5-6):

- What would you want to contribute that outlasts your lifetime?
- What skills/knowledge/resources do you have that could serve others?
- What problems in the world genuinely bother you that you now have resources to address them?

Approach 3: Energy-Based Assessment

Tends to appeal to Closers who trust gut instincts and immediate feedback.

This approach is rooted in positive psychology research showing that sustained energy and flow states indicate values alignment.

Energy Mapping (Weeks 1-2):

- Review your calendar from 6 months before exit planning and rate how each major activity/meeting would have made you feel (1-10 energy scale).

- Which people in your life increase your energy? Which decreases it?

- When in your life have you felt most "alive" and authentic to yourself? What were you doing?

Values Archaeology (Weeks 3-4):

- What did you love doing before you needed to make money from it?

- What activities make you lose track of time completely?

- What accomplishments are you most proud of that had nothing to do with financial rewards?

Energy-Aligned Design (Weeks 5-6):

- If you never had to worry about money again, what would you spend your time doing?

- What would you do even if no one ever recognised or thanked you for it?

- How could you restructure your life to maximise high-energy, values-aligned time?

Approach 4: Past, Present, Future Reflection

Tends to appeal to Equity Earners who prefer systematic, comprehensive analysis.

This approach uses narrative therapy techniques – examining your life story to understand how values have evolved and should continue evolving.

Past Values (Weeks 1-2):

- What were you willing to endure or sacrifice for in your 20s that you wouldn't tolerate today?

- Looking back at your biggest regrets, what values were you ignoring when you made those decisions?
- What advice did you reject earlier in life that you now wish you had followed?

Present Reality Check (Weeks 3-4):

- If someone followed you around for a month and watched your choices, what would they conclude you value most?
- What do you find yourself defending or justifying to others, and what does that reveal about conflicting values?
- When do you feel like you're pretending to be someone you're not, and what authentic values are being suppressed?

Future Design (Weeks 5-6):

- What would you want written about you in your obituary beyond business achievements?
- If you could only influence three people for the rest of your life, who would they be and how?
- What would your 80-year-old self tell you to prioritise right now?

If you commit to this work, you'll be pursuing **genuine fulfilment after financial success.** Skipping values recalibration will result in repeating the same patterns of misery from the past, just with more money.

As someone once said,

> *"Money doesn't buy you happiness;*
> *it just buys you a better class of misery."*

Carnegie figured this out over a century ago. He did the hard work of examining what actually mattered to him once survival wasn't the issue. That conscious choice to recalibrate his values from accumulation to contribution transformed not just how he spent his money, but how he spent his *life*.

The preceding values work is the foundation. And it will help inform the destination.

Once you're clear on what drives you, the next question becomes: what does meaningful work look like when you're operating from these new values? What do you do with the clarity, freedom, and resources you now have?

That's where your second mountain comes in.

✔ CHECKPOINT: VET YOUR VALUES

- Are you conceptualising future success like a first-time founder?
- What is the gap between what you say is important, and what you actually prioritise?
- Are you chasing numbers that no longer serve you?
- Have you imagined what impact your exit could set in motion?
- Now that you're financially free; what genuinely energises you? What drains you?

CHAPTER 16

The Second Mountain

"We make a living by what we get,
but we make a life by what we give."

– Winston Churchill

THE MYTH OF THE FINISH LINE

There's a dangerously seductive narrative in entrepreneurial culture: build, exit, retire. Work hard, get rich, then enjoy the fruits of your labour for the rest of your days.

It's a narrative that fails almost every founder who achieves it.

What most successful founders eventually discover is that the human spirit needs more than leisure and consumption to thrive. We need purpose, challenge, growth, and meaningful contribution.

The finish line mentality creates a particular kind of post-exit trap: if your exit represents the end of your story, what happens in the chapters after it? Many founders find themselves stuck in an existential epilogue, unsure how to create meaning in what feels like bonus time.

The most fulfilled founders I know treat their exit differently. It's not the end of their story – it's the beginning of a new chapter **with better resources.**

THE POWER OF THE SECOND MOUNTAIN

Psychologist Carl Jung first identified this pattern back in 1931. He described life as having two distinct phases: the first half focused on building ego, establishing identity, and achieving external success. The second half involves transcending that ego-driven approach to find deeper meaning and purpose.

Author David Brooks later popularised this concept using the metaphor of two mountains. The first mountain is about achievement, acquisition, and external success – building your business, achieving financial independence, gaining recognition. Founders can spend decades ascending this first mountain.

The second mountain is different. It's about contribution, connection, and meaning beyond yourself. Less about what you can get and more about what you can give. Less about achievement and more about purpose.

For many founders, the exit creates the opportunity – and sometimes the necessity – to begin climbing this second mountain.

. . . .

Tony Falkenstein ONZM, a "richlister" who built and sold multiple successful businesses in New Zealand, describes this shift: "On my first mountain, success was measured by financial outcomes and growth metrics. On my second mountain, success is measured by impact – how many lives I can positively influence through my work with young entrepreneurs and educational initiatives."

This shift in perspective transforms the exit from an ending into a beginning.

This phase is not retirement, but reinvention.

FINDING YOUR SECOND MOUNTAIN

Unlike the earlier challenge of climbing the mountain of your building and ultimate exit, the most challenging aspect of the second mountain isn't climbing it – it's finding the right mountain to climb.

From experience, I know that after years of singular focus on my business, the sudden freedom to pursue anything was (paradoxically) paralysing. With unlimited options come unlimited questions: What should I do next? What am I truly passionate about? Where can I create the most value?

Those who navigate this transition most successfully approach it not as a single decision, but as an intentional exploration – a process of discovery guided by reflection, experimentation, and self-awareness.

Some founders throw themselves into angel investing, finding energy in helping other entrepreneurs navigate familiar challenges. Others discover they love teaching – turns out all that hard-won wisdom means something when shared with people who can use it. A few become serial entrepreneurs again, but with completely different motivations. Building around problems they care about rather than markets they can dominate.

I've watched founders discover their thing through volunteering at their kids' schools, through travel that opened their eyes to problems they never knew existed, through finally having real conversations with their spouses about what they both wanted from life.

Your second mountain doesn't have to look like anyone else's. Maybe it's being present for your family in ways you never could before. Maybe it's mastering something you always wanted to learn but never had bandwidth for. Maybe it's applying your skills to problems in your community that no one else has the resources or experience to tackle properly.

The beauty of this phase isn't what you choose – it's that you finally get to **choose deliberately** rather than by default.

THE EXPERIMENTATION PHASE

Selling your business is like going through a divorce –- you've been heading along a familiar path for years, and now that path has fundamentally changed. Everything you thought you knew about what motivates you, what success looks like, and how you want to spend your time is suddenly up for question.

As we covered in the previous chapter, until you've done the values work and landed comfortably on what drives you now, the smart approach is to make a range of small bets and avoid any big commitments.

This is where minimum viable proposition thinking becomes crucial. Instead of jumping into a massive new venture or writing a huge cheque to a cause or startup, **start small.**

Join one non-profit board; don't chair three. Mentor a couple of founders; don't launch an accelerator. Make a few small angel investments; don't become a full-time VC. The approach that works is giving yourself permission to explore multiple paths simultaneously while keeping your commitments deliberately small.

Teach one university course while volunteering a few hours per month in your community. Try some angel investing while exploring problems you want to solve. Over time, patterns emerge. One path will consistently energise you, while others feel like obligations. One type of contribution will feel natural, while others require constant effort. One way of helping will make you lose track of time, while others make you check your watch.

Those who navigate this phase successfully treat it kind of like market research on themselves. They experiment with genuine curiosity, but without betting the farm on early hypotheses. They give themselves permission to explore, to fail, and to change direction as they discover what truly resonates. The key is resisting the founder impulse to go big immediately. As I've suggested, our values have shifted. I'd highly encourage taking the time to discover what they've shifted toward.

FROM ACHIEVEMENT TO IMPACT

Once you've found your second mountain through experimentation, how you keep score starts to shift.

As I mentioned with Ambit, I measured success the way founders usually do – and investors want to see: revenue, valuation, market share, exit multiples. The scoreboard was pretty simple: more money meant more success.

Then I had those exits. The old metrics stopped making sense.

Once you have enough money – and "enough" is different for everyone, but you'll know when you get there – the traditional metrics become meaningless. Revenue, profit margins, share price... these numbers that once drove every decision start to feel hollow.

You have to consciously decide to start keeping score differently. But once you do, the game becomes infinitely more interesting.

Tony Falkenstein talks about the entrepreneurs he's mentored and the impact they're creating. Not the returns on his angel investments –the **actual human impact** of the founders he's helped succeed.

Founders in my orbit who experienced a deep sense of satisfaction and accomplishment post-exit started asking completely different questions. *How many people did I help? What problems did I solve that mattered? What did I create that will outlast me?*

I repeat: your exit number will be forgotten. The story you write with what it affords you won't be.

RECONSTRUCTING YOUR IDENTITY

One of the most profound challenges of the second mountain is reconstructing your identity after having identified so thoroughly with your founder role.

As we've now explored at length, for many founders, their business becomes more than what they do – it becomes who they are. Your sense of self becomes deeply intertwined with your role, your company, and your industry. When the exit removes these identity anchors, many founders experience what psychologists call "identity foreclosure" – a collapse of self-concept that can lead to depression, anxiety, or existential crisis.

The founders who thrive post-exit approach this not as identity loss, but as identity evolution – an opportunity to develop a more expansive and authentic sense of self that transcends any single role or achievement.

From role to purpose

The most successful identity transitions involve shifting from role-based identity ("I am a CEO") to purpose-based identity ("I develop solutions to problems that matter"). This shift creates **psychological continuity** through the transition while opening space for **new expressions of your core purpose.**

What you truly love probably isn't being a CEO specifically – it's likely solving complex challenges and developing people's capabilities. Once you understand that, you can see multiple ways to express that same purpose in your next chapter, from consulting to teaching to writing. **Your identity expands rather than contracts.**

Building a multi-dimensional self

As a founder, your identity was one-dimensional by necessity. The business demanded everything, and other parts of you went dormant. After selling, you can rekindle other aspects of who you are – artist, mentor, investor, community leader. You're not just "former CEO of X company" – you become a multidimensional person with many ways of creating value and finding meaning.

Giving back (without creating new headaches)

Many founders naturally gravitate toward philanthropy as their second mountain. There's something appealing about using your wealth and skills to solve problems that matter. But be careful not to recreate the same patterns that made you miserable in business.

I learned this the hard way when I started a charity. My intention was sound – I wanted to reinvent how the philanthropy sector operated. But what I created was another gigantic headache for myself. I was trying to build something from scratch, optimise for metrics that didn't really matter to me, and convince other people to fund my vision.

Sound familiar?

The most fulfilled founders I know approach giving back with the same conscious awareness they bring to their values work. They ask: what am I trying to achieve here? Am I solving a problem I genuinely care about, or am I just creating another vehicle for my achievement addiction?

Some write cheques to existing organisations doing work they believe in. Others get hands-on with causes in their communities. A few apply their specific skills – like systems thinking or scaling operations – to help non-profits become more effective.

The key is understanding what type of contribution energises you rather than defaulting to "starting a foundation" because that's what successful people are supposed to do.

Your philanthropy should reflect your recalibrated values, not recreate your old patterns with a charitable tax deduction.

THE QUESTION NOBODY ASKS

After exploring all these possibilities – experimenting with different paths, finding your second mountain, shifting how you measure success – there's one question left that rarely gets asked in all the exit advice and post-success planning.

What if the best exit strategy is no exit at all?

Founders tend to assume the goal is to build something valuable and then sell it. But once you've done the values work, once you understand what drives you, once you've seen how the scorecard changes after financial success, a different possibility emerges.

Maybe the company you've built, operating from your newly clarified values, deployed toward problems you care about, could be more valuable in your hands than anyone else's.

Maybe your second mountain isn't something new you build after you exit. Maybe it's what your current business becomes when you stop optimising for other people's metrics and start optimising for your own.

It's a question worth asking before you sign the papers.

✔ CHECKPOINT: FOR LOVE AND MONEY

- What did you love most about building your business that had nothing to do with money?

- When you think about the next 10 years, what would make you feel genuinely excited to get up in the morning?

- What problems in the world bother you enough that you'd want to spend your own time and money solving them?

- Are you designing your second mountain around your actual values, or just recreating familiar patterns with different labels?

- If you could only be remembered for one thing beyond your business success, what would you want it to be?

"True wealth is the ability to fully experience life."

– Henry David Thoreau

CHAPTER 17

Why You Should Keep Your Company

"When you're finally wealthy, you'll realise it wasn't what you were seeking in the first place."

– Eric Jorgenson, Jack Butcher, and Tim Ferriss

THE EXIT MYTH: WHY SELLING ISN'T ALWAYS THE WIN

We've spent this whole book talking about exits – designing them, negotiating them, maximising them. It's time for me to be the contrarian:

You don't have to sell.

Not now. Not ever.

Selling your company can be an incredible milestone. It can change your life. But it's not the only version of success – and it's definitely not the only path to freedom.

In fact, for a lot of founders, keeping your business is the smartest, richest, and most fulfilling move you can make.

After 16 chapters of exit strategy, here's the strategy of not exiting at all.

The mythology around exits

The mythology around exits runs deep in entrepreneurial culture. We celebrate acquisitions on the covers of business magazines. We track "exit values" as scorecards of success. Venture capitalists and startup communities hold up the exit as the ultimate validation of a founder's journey.

This cultural bias creates enormous pressure to sell – even when it may not be the right decision for your specific situation. This whole book is about exits, which only reinforces how deeply embedded this thinking is in our community.

Not every business should be built to sell

The standard entrepreneurial advice today is "build to sell" – create a business that's systematised, less dependent on you, with clean financials and clear growth potential.

This is excellent advice for creating a valuable, well-run company. But building a sellable business gives you the *option* to sell – it doesn't obligate you to do so.

The problem with defaulting to exit

In the startup echo chamber, exits are seen as the finish line, the badge of honour, the ultimate validation. Founders who exit are applauded. Founders who stay? Often forgotten.

Too many founders drift toward exit because they're tired, bored, frustrated, or externally pressured. They think they've peaked. Or they've hit a wall. Or they're comparing themselves to others who've exited.

But those aren't good reasons to sell. Those are good reasons to pause, reassess, and possibly redesign how you run the business. Because the worst outcome isn't missing an exit – it's exiting for the wrong reasons, then realising too late that you gave up your life's work prematurely.

I was traveling for business in Kathmandu, and through my various connections there I observed a stark difference in thinking and operating businesses. Many businesses were being run by 3rd, 4th and occasionally 5th generation families. And the consequences were astounding:

- Incredible stewardship and vision continuity
- Huge, robust, and impactful businesses
- Immense wealth creation
- OK, and some reasonable sibling conflict. But that's for another time.

The contrast was striking. While we obsess over exit timelines, these families think in decades and generations. You don't need to sell your company to be successful. You need to build something worth keeping. That generational thinking in Kathmandu wasn't just about culture – it was about understanding how real wealth compounds over time.

COMPOUNDING WEALTH VS. ONE-TIME LIQUIDITY

From a purely financial perspective, holding a great business often creates significantly more wealth than selling it. This isn't just theory – it's mathematics.

The power of compounding returns

When you sell your business, you exchange **future uncertain returns for present certain cash.** While this reduces risk, it also caps your upside precisely when your business may be entering its most valuable growth phase.

The math is straightforward: a business growing at 20% annually will double in value every 3.6 years. A diversified investment portfolio might return 7-10% annually. Over time, that difference compounds dramatically.

This mathematical reality applies to businesses across industries. Compounding growth within a business you control often outperforms the returns available in public markets or other passive investments.

Cash flow: the overlooked wealth builder

Beyond equity value, ongoing business ownership provides another powerful wealth-building tool: **consistent cash flow.**

A profitable business can fund your desired lifestyle without touching principal, invest in other opportunities, support causes you care about, and reinvest selectively for further growth.

This dual benefit – growing equity value plus ongoing cash flow – creates wealth-building potential that a one-time exit often cannot match.

Most founders who have a large exit event go back to doing something to generate cash flow within two to five years. Lifestyle creep happens faster than expected, and suddenly, they're making large purchases while discovering that life is more expensive than they anticipated. When you keep your business, you maintain that cash flow engine instead of having to rebuild it later.

Freedom without selling

Perhaps the most compelling reason to sell your business is the freedom it promises – freedom from day-to-day responsibilities, freedom to pursue new interests, freedom from financial constraints. What if you could achieve this freedom **without giving up ownership?** What if you could design your business to deliver exit-like benefits while you **continue to own and guide it?**

The owner-investor model

Many successful founders have transitioned from operator-owners to investor-owners – maintaining ownership while fundamentally changing their relationship with the business. This model – where you own but don't operate day-to-day – delivers many exit-like benefits: dramatically reduced time commitment, freedom from operational stress, financial independence through ongoing distributions, continued equity appreciation, and maintenance of purpose and impact.

BUILDING A FREEDOM-FOCUSED BUSINESS

Creating this freedom-without-selling environment requires intentional business design around several key elements:

- **Leadership Development**: Building a leadership team capable of running the business without your daily involvement. This often requires investing in recruitment, training, and appropriate incentive structures.

- **Systems and Process Documentation**: Codifying how your business operates reduces dependency on any individual, including you. This creates resilience and transferability of knowledge.

- **Role Redesign:** Perhaps most importantly, you must deliberately redesign your own role to focus on your unique contributions, while delegating everything else.
- **Financial Alignment:** Creating clear profit-sharing, distribution policies, and governance structures ensures your business serves your financial goals without requiring your constant attention.

The goal here is to design a business where your involvement adds demonstrable value, rather than being needed at the wheelhouse day-to-day and week-to-week.

THE EMOTIONAL & IDENTITY UPSIDE OF STAYING

Beyond financial considerations, there are profound emotional and identity benefits to continuing to own your business – benefits that often go unrecognised in exit-focused discussions.

Purpose, impact, and meaning

For many founders, their business represents their primary vehicle for creating impact and expressing their purpose. Selling can create a significant meaning vacuum that proves difficult to fill.

This purpose-driven perspective recognises that a successful business represents more than financial value – it's a mechanism for materialising your vision in the world.

Legacy and long-term thinking

Continued ownership allows for **multi-generational thinking** and **legacy creation** that selling often precludes.

This long-term orientation – building for decades rather than for an exit – enables different conversations (and ultimately, decisions) about investment, culture, and strategy that often create both deeper meaning and superior long-term outcomes.

The joy of mastery and evolution

Many founders discover that continued ownership allows for the profound satisfaction that comes from ongoing mastery and evolution.

This perspective recognises that building and growing a company represents a unique learning laboratory – one that continues to provide growth opportunities even after the initial building phase.

FALSE POSITIVES: WHEN YOU THINK YOU WANT TO SELL (BUT DON'T)

Sometimes what feels like "I need to exit this business" is actually "I need to exit this version of my role." Before you assume selling is the answer, check whether you're experiencing one of these false positives:

1. Role Misalignment: You're doing work that doesn't match your strengths or interests – stuck in operations when you love strategy, trapped in admin when you want to build, or handling tasks that should be delegated. The business isn't the problem; your job description is.

2. The Control Trap: You've become the bottleneck for everything. Every decision goes through you; you can't step away; the business depends too heavily on your daily involvement. You're not ready to sell – you're ready to delegate.

3. External Optimisation: You're running the business to please others – investors, advisors, industry expectations – instead of designing it around what energises and fulfils you. The solution isn't selling; it's reclaiming control of your priorities.

4. Growth Without Evolution: Your role hasn't evolved as the business has grown. You're still doing founder-of-10-people work in a 100-person company. The business outgrew your role, but that doesn't mean you should exit – it means you should redesign.

DESIGNING A HOLD STRATEGY

If you decide to keep your business, don't just default into it. **Be intentional about how you'll make it work.**

Take some money off the table

Just because you're not selling doesn't mean you can't get some liquidity. Set up regular distributions so you're not reinvesting every penny back into the business. You've earned the right to enjoy some of the wealth you've created.

Another option is a partial sell-down – selling a portion of the company to bring in an external investor. This gives you immediate liquidity while keeping control. Often, these investors can take on operational roles too, which helps with the next point.

Redesign your role and set boundaries

Figure out what parts of running the business you enjoy and delegate the rest. You're the owner – **you get to choose what your job looks like.** Decide how much time you want to spend on the business and stick to it. Otherwise, you'll end up recreating the same problems that made you consider selling in the first place.

Keep your options open

Run the business like you might sell it someday, even if you don't plan to. Clean financials, good systems, strong team. This keeps doors open and makes the business more valuable, regardless of whether you sell or keep it.

The real success: optionality

This entire book hasn't been about selling. It's been about **building optionality.**

If you reach the point where you could sell – but don't have to – you've already won.

If buyers come knocking, and you can say "maybe" – that's power.

The real goal isn't selling. It's building something valuable, enduring, and self-sustaining.

And maybe the most satisfying legacy of all is to say: "I built this. I still own this. And I still love it."

Tony Falkenstein put it perfectly: "When I stop enjoying the game, I'll stop playing it."

But until then?

Keep playing. Keep building. Keep owning.

The choice is yours.

✔ FINAL CHECKPOINT FOR PART IV
TO SELL OR NOT TO SELL, THAT IS THE
QUESTION.

- What aspects of running your business do you genuinely love versus what feels like obligation?
- Are you considering selling because you want to, or because you think you should?
- What would need to change about how you work for you to fall in love with your business again?
- If you took a 6-week sabbatical and came back refreshed, would you still want to sell?
- What would you regret more: keeping the business and missing an exit opportunity, or selling and watching someone else build what you started?

We started this book **assuming you wanted to exit.**

We're ending it with the possibility that the best exit strategy might be **no exit at all.**

The goal was never to convince you one way or the other. It was to make sure whatever you choose, you choose it deliberately. Whether you sell for $50 million or keep building for the next 20 years, make that choice from a position of **strength, clarity,** and **genuine preference.**

That's the difference between exit by design and exit by default.

The choice, as always, is **yours.**

As the Alcoholics Anonymous founder Bill W. stated,

"The only freedom a human being can ever know is doing what you ought to do because you want to do it."

Epilogue

You've made it this far. **Congratulations!** Most people who buy business books never make it past chapter one – they just have a pile of guilt sitting on the bedside table. Frankly, I shouldn't be surprised, and neither should you. You built a business and took it to the point where exit is a real possibility. Finishing what you start is clearly part of your DNA.

Navigating the choppy waters of starting and building a business is one of life's greatest teachers. You'll have grown so much from successfully navigating those challenges. But building the business is different to selling it. Once you're successful, you'll face an **entirely different set of questions.**

I learned this the hard way with Ambit. I was clear in my intentions at the outset – build something meaningful, create value, maintain control over my own destiny. But somewhere along the way, I got lost in the vanity metrics and the omnipresent pursuit of growth for growth's sake, confusing others' objectives as my own. The tech press always loved our story because from the outside, it looked like success.

From the inside? **It felt hollow.** I'd accidentally traded my original vision for someone else's definition of winning.

When I finally stopped the think about it properly, it was clear: I was living to a set of values that simply lacked currency.

Whether or not you know it, life will be different after your exit – but in ways you perhaps didn't anticipate. The money is important until you have it, and it's really an entry ticket to a much more interesting question:

How are you going to design this next phase of your life,
and what are you going to make it all mean?

This book was really about building optionality – the power to choose whether to sell or stay based on what serves you, not what entrepreneurial culture expects. Whether that choice leads to a strategic sale, a family succession, or continuing to own what you've created, make that decision deliberately.

Exit by design, not by default.

And don't stop here. If you haven't already done the values exercise from earlier in the book, **do it now.** That single exercise will serve you more than any valuation multiple or deal structure.

If this journey has resonated with you, I'd love to continue the conversation. Find me on LinkedIn, visit my website, sign up for my newsletter, and have a listen to my weekly podcast, 2 Commas.

The next piece of work where you define your version of freedom is where the story gets fascinating.

The question isn't whether you can build something valuable. **You've already proven that.**

I reckon the question is:

What will you do with that value once you have it?

The exit isn't the end of the story. It's the start of a chapter only you can write. So make your move, but **make it yours.**

Notes

1   See "The Untold Toll' by Startup Snapshot" – https://www.
    startupsnapshot.com/research/the-untold-toll-the-impact-of-
    stress-on-the-well-being-of-startup-founders-and-ceos/; "More
    than half of founders experienced burnout last year" by Sifted
    – https://sifted.eu/articles/founders-mental-health-2025; and
    "(Founder) Burnout" by b2venture – https://resources.b2venture.
    vc/hr/founder-burnout.

2   See "The Significant Objects Project" at https://significantobjects.
    com/.

3   See "Don't Make This Common M&A Mistake" by Graham Kenny
    at https://hbr.org/2020/03/dont-make-this-common-ma-mistake,
    and "The Big Idea: The New M&A Playbook" by Clayton M.
    Christensen, Richard Alton, Curtis Rising and Andrew Waldeck at
    https://hbr.org/2011/03/the-big-idea-the-new-ma-playbook

4   See "Your acquired hires are leaving. Here's why" by Meredith
    Somers at https://mitsloan.mit.edu/ideas-made-to-matter/
    your-acquired-hires-are-leaving-heres-why.

5   See "The Art and Science of Earnouts in M&A"
    at https://corpgov.law.harvard.edu/2025/07/11/
    the-art-and-science-of-earn-outs-in-ma/

6   See "Customer Retention Statistics By Industry 2025" at https://
    www.demandsage.com/customer-retention-statistics/

Reviews of **2 Commas**

"Most founders think they're building companies. What they're really building are identities – and those can be the hardest things to sell. *2 Commas* is part business guide, part mirror. It's uncomfortably honest, and that's exactly why it works.

I don't usually enjoy business books, but this one isn't about spreadsheets or valuations – it's about the mind of the founder. Josh turns the mess of ego, identity, and ambition into something practical, funny, and genuinely useful. Even if you never sell a business, it'll make you rethink what success really costs."

Jimi Hunt – Bestselling Author of *A Bit Mental*.

"Josh has created something rare: a guide that's both deeply practical and genuinely wise. His writing is punchy, clear, and feels like sitting across the table from someone who's been through it all and knows exactly what you need to hear. This is the resource every founder needs when facing the biggest decision of their professional life – honest, actionable, and completely grounded in reality."

Suzi McAlpine – Bestselling Author of *Beyond Burnout*. Speaker, Coach, Director.

"Josh understands what many advisors overlook; private company exits are fundamentally human transactions. The numbers matter, but the people matter more. In this insightful book, Josh expertly navigates the emotional, strategic, and deeply personal reality of selling your company – with the wisdom of someone who's been in the room when everything is on the line."

Neil Millar – Strategic M+A Advisor

"For every founder who thinks about eventually exiting his/her business, Josh Comrie's book is a source of profound and practical knowledge. Josh's four dimensions of a strategic exit lay out a set of frameworks, methodologies, mindsets, and perspectives, as well as tools and processes, in a highly engaging manner. It is evident that his knowledge is grounded in profound experience, which is highly valuable."

Marc Stockli – Global Chair, Entrepreneurs Organisation. 2 Comma-exited founder.

"Ever since I started investing in startups nearly 20 years ago, I've been struck by how much investors talk about exits – and how little we actually know about them. Except Josh. He's built a vast store of knowledge by doing it himself (more than once) and by talking endlessly to founders about their exits on his unmissable *2 Commas* podcast.

Now he's written the book. A practical guide for founders – not just on how to answer investor questions about exits, but more importantly, how to proactively plan your own exit from the beginning.

The magic question – 'how will this all end?' – is something I wish I'd asked when I started my business. 2 Commas is the playbook for founders who want to answer that question themselves and plan their own exit on their own terms. Read it."

Debra Hall – Founder, Research Solutions – now Investor, Advisor and Director

"Josh's account here is an illuminating journey of the rollercoaster ride that is becoming an entrepreneur, exiting, and defining new purpose. I was one of the lucky ones to get out the other side with my mental and physical health intact – Josh was a powerful mentor (and friend) who witnessed it all"

Matt Chapman – Founder, Nine-figure+ professional services exit.

"It's super rare to come across a business book that feels genuinely new. Josh nails the emotional journey of selling your company—something most founders only do once—and helps you approach it with clarity and confidence. I wish I'd had this when I was going through my own exit."

Trent Mankelow – Investor, Director, and Advisor.
Founder of two 2 Comma exited companies.

"*2 Commas* is immensely readable, offering lessons in business illustrated with real-world examples. If you're in business, this is a must-read. If you're thinking of going into business, it's a must-read. And if you've already retired from business, it's a must-read on how you should have done it. Entrepreneurs are like four-year-olds — they believe they know everything and can do it all themselves. Sometimes 'Mum and Dad' need to step in to show them otherwise. This book is that 'Mum and Dad' for entrepreneurs."

Tony Falkenstein, CNZM – Founder and Chief Exec – Just Life Group.
Dozens of exits!

"*2 Commas* is exactly what founders need before they exit. Every message is clear, every principle is practical, and the content is organized in a way that actually makes sense. I wish we'd had this during our exit – it would have helped us navigate the process and what came after. If you're building something you might sell, read this book."

Marisa Fong – Entrepreneur, Director, Speaker, and Mentor.
The largest recruitment company exit in NZ's history.

"With *2 Commas*, Josh has distilled dozens of experiences and decades of learnings into one excellent, accessible resource. This book had me nodding from the very first page and is a must-read for anyone starting, scaling, or exiting a business."

Janine Grainger – EasyCrypto Founder and Exiter.

Josh Comrie

Building Value. Creating Freedom.

I work with founders and business owners who've built something valuable and want to **extract that value intelligently** – whether through strategic transformation, succession, or exit. My practice brings clarity to strategy, strengthens execution, and turns operations into intelligent assets that lift valuation and liberate founders. Over the course of an engagement, my aim is simple: to propel your business into the upper quartile of valuations and add one to two points to your EBIT multiple.

I've founded and exited multiple companies, built a portfolio of 50+ angel investments (including a 199× return), and hold an extensive industrial property portfolio. I understand what it takes - because I've done it.

I can help you with:

- **Advisory partnerships** – long-term, embedded engagements that help founders build value and freedom simultaneously.

- **Exit strategy & preparation** – getting your business ready for sale and navigating the process with clarity.

- **Keynote speaking** – conferences or symposiums; I speak on entrepreneurship, wealth creation, connection and succession.

Host of 2 Commas Podcast

New Zealand's #1 business podcast on entrepreneurship & exits
~30,000 weekly listeners | 1 million+ downloads in the first 12 months